EDDIE WEINSTEIN

17 Days in Treblinka

Daring to Resist, and Refusing to Die

Eddie Weinstein

17 Days in Treblinka

Daring to Resist, and Refusing to Die

Edited by
Noah Lasman

Yad Vashem Publications • Jerusalem • 2008

Translated from the Hebrew by Naftali Greenwood
Language Editor: Lenn Schramm
Production Editor: Avital Saf

First edition: Quenched Steel, 2002

Second edition: Quenched Steel, 2005

Third edition: Quenched Steel, 2007

Fourth edition: 17 Days in Treblinka, 2008

Fifth edition: 17 Days in Treblinka, 2009

ISBN: 978-965-308-321-9

Originally published as *Plada Rotahat,* 2001

Printed by Offset Nathan Shlomo Press
Jerusalem, Israel

Contents

Preface

I have told my story in chronological order, as I remember what happened to me, my parents, my brother, my uncles and aunts, and around forty first cousins.

I cannot explain the nature of the occurrences and decisions that I retell here; I leave it to readers to draw the conclusions.

I dedicate this book to my late mother, murdered in Treblinka; to my father, who died in New York in 1972; to my brother Srulik (Israel) and to my cousin Chaim Brukmann, who helped my brother hide me in the clothing of the dead. My brother and Chaim were murdered in Treblinka.

Eddie Weinstein

The fish pond and the little forest where the author was hiding for 20 months

The author's family from left to right:
Daniel, Jesse, Johnathan, Sarah, Jordan, grandma Judith, the author, Hannah, Suzanne, Paula, Larry, Michael and Joshua.

Łosice

I was born in Łosice, a town in Siedlce County, Poland, about eleven miles west of the River Bug. The Brukmanns, my mother's family, had lived in that area for generations. My mother, Leah, was the youngest of five children and the only daughter. She married my father in 1912, when she was about twenty years old.

My father, Asher Weinstein, was born in Bejdy, a village about ten miles from Łosice. He served in the Tsar's army for three and a half years. Although he had learned tailoring in his youth, I do not recall that he ever practiced that trade except when he sewed or repaired clothing for members of his family. Since my father found it impossible to support his family as a tailor, he went into business. He went out into the nearby villages in a horsecart and bought eggs, hens, ducks, and geese from the peasants, for resale in town. In the summer, he would rent an orchard and a one or two-room house where the family would live.

My brother Srulik (Israel), born in 1926, was two years younger than me. When I was three or four I was enrolled in a *cheder* — a religious school for boys of that age — which the *melamed* (teacher) ran in his own apartment.

The apartment had a small kitchen and a large room that served as living room, bedroom, and classroom. The children sat on two benches on either side of a long table that ran down the center of the room; the *melamed* sat at one end, facing the children. For a weekly fee he taught us the Hebrew alphabet and the prayers. I started public school when I was six, but continued to go to the *cheder* in the afternoon.

When I was in fifth grade, I was severely ill for about ten weeks, after which I had to learn to walk all over again. Later I studied in the yeshiva in Łosice. In October 1938, when I was fifteen, I went to work for Moshe Goldstein, who owned the only wholesale store in town. My salary was a paltry five zlotys for an eighty-hour week. I was happy anyway, because there were very few jobs to be had in Łosice.

In March 1939, I looked out through the store's glass door and saw a man running, followed by a crowd of children and adults. When the man stopped at a public notice board my employer, Moshe Goldstein, sent me out to see what was happening. The man had posted a notice that the Polish army was calling up the reserves. The whole town was upset by the news. After about an hour of silence, one could hear the sobbing of wives and mothers whose husbands and sons had to report for active service. It seemed as if everyone was wailing. I saw small groups forming in the market square. What's happening? people asked each other. What's the world coming to?

At about 10 P.M., peasants from neighboring villages arrived with horsecarts to transport the reservists to the rendezvous points established by the Polish army. The men sang army songs as they left town.

The older men began to return about three months later. Another three months passed and then, on September 1, 1939, Nazi Germany invaded Poland. World War II had begun. On Saturday, September 9, the Germans bombarded our town. The great synagogue was destroyed, about fifty people were killed, and many others were wounded. Most of the townspeople fled for their lives; no one was left behind at the clinic to treat the many casualties.

My family fled to Bejdy, where my father's two sisters and brother lived. We spent about six days with them and then returned home. Several days later, advance companies of German troops arrived on motorcycles and launched a wave of violence and pillage. People aged forty or more, who remembered the events of World War I, regarded this as a matter of routine — what the victors always do; they hoped and expected that life would eventually go back to normal.

The German motorcyclists left town the same day. A few days later, two armored vehicles packed with German soldiers pulled into Łosice and stopped in the market square. The soldiers raided the shops for valuables before withdrawing to the edge of town. These incursions continued for about ten days.

Rumor had it that Germany and Russia had agreed to establish a new border along the River Vistula. Russian soldiers arrived several days later. They behaved quite amiably. The younger men flirted with local girls, got into arguments with local teenagers, and proclaimed the superiority of the Soviet regime over ours. Peasants were told that land would be redistributed; townspeople were told that industry would be developed and everyone would have equal opportunity in property and schooling.

The young Jews eagerly absorbed the stories of the Russians, who asserted that in their vast country all people were equal in every respect. The hopes of generations of Jews were finally about to come true. Rallies were held. The Soviet officers told us that they intended to stay; the Red Army never retreated from a place it had occupied. A new town council was formed, under a new mayor, and a militia was established.

A soldier played the accordion in the market square and a few people danced to his music. We enjoyed the situation for the few days that it lasted.

One evening, however, a new rumor spread: the Russians were withdrawing eastward to the River Bug. That meant the Germans would return. Łosice was gripped by panic, particularly in light of reports about the Germans' behavior in the county seat, Siedlce, about nineteen miles away. People said that the Germans had ordered representatives of the Jews to report to the town hall, where they were beaten, kicked, and thrown down the stairs. Several needed assistance to get back home; all had their faces bloodied.

The new frontier was about 12.5 miles from Łosice. Several townspeople packed their belongings and followed the retreating Russians over the River Bug. Many young people also walked in that direction. My mother asked my cousins to take me with them but they refused, however, because they did not wish to take on the extra responsibility.

My brother Israel cried and pleaded with my parents to leave town and cross the river to the Russian side. The exodus would have been much greater had the nearby forest not swarmed with Polish gangs who robbed Jews of their belongings. We were told that even those who had managed to cross to the other side of the Bug found it hard to find housing and work there. Many returned to their homes. The war would not last long, they declared; Poland did surrender, but Germany would fall to the British and the French in short order. The Soviet authorities soon defined those who did not go back home as security risks and exiled them to the forests of Siberia. Meanwhile, the Germans returned to Łosice. They announced that they were going to establish a new order that would last for a thousand years.

One day, an SS *Obersturmführer* showed up in Łosice to serve as military governor, or Kommandant. At first he walked in the market square and kicked or punched anyone who failed to doff his hat as he passed. Later, pedestrians got into the habit of ducking into side streets whenever they saw him approaching.

One night in December 1939, the Germans arrested six Jews and one Christian, led them to the outskirts of town, and murdered them. People said that somebody had informed the Germans that the victims' children had embraced Communism and left town with the Russians. The next day, a notice with the names of the murdered people was posted in the market square, announcing that they had been executed.

The Germans then established a Judenrat (Jewish council), independent of the Polish municipal authorities, to govern the Jewish population. The Judenrat conscripted Jews for public works, some necessary and others not. The Germans seized the opportunity to abuse and torture the frailer workers.

Thousands of refugees and deportees from Western Poland packed the town, doubling its population. The municipal authorities dealt with the Poles and resettled them in nearby villages; Jewish refugees, in contrast, became wards of their own people. Housing density soon became unbearable. The newcomers had to share not only dwellings but also kitchen utensils and food with the locals. Efforts began to procure food for those who were starving.

A German gendarmerie, known as the Schutzpolizei (Schupo for short), entered Łosice in February 1940 and established their headquarters above the pharmacy across the street from our house.

Each month the Germans announced new and more severe restrictions against the Jews. First, Jews were ordered to wear bands with a Star of David on their right arm. Next, their right to travel out of town was limited and they were subjected to a more stringent curfew than that applying to Poles. Still later, Jewish merchants and artisans were forbidden to ply their trades and more and more Jews were conscripted for slave labor.

In August 1940, the Wehrmacht requisitioned 400

Jews for labor at the Niemojki railroad station, about three miles from town. I received an order, signed by the chairman of the Judenrat, to report to Niemojki the next day. The job involved building a concrete platform more than 500 yards long, laying several railroad tracks, and constructing a spur to allow trains to turn around. It was grueling labor. The Germans, evidently facing an inflexible deadline, pushed us to our limits, and we completed the work by the end of February 1941. This was the second station near the Russian frontier. In June 1941 the Germans used it to move weapons up to the front for the attack on the Soviet Union.

In March 1941, after my work in Niemojki was completed, I was ordered to report to Mrozy, about fifty-six miles from home. This was a railroad station near the town of Kalushin, about nineteen miles from Warsaw. Fifty young men from Łosice, including myself, were sent there. We worked a twelve-hour shift through the night, starting at 6 P.M., quarrying stone from a mountain and laying tracks. We slept in an unheated freight car. Many workers, myself among them, suffered frostbitten legs.

We loaded mud onto small freight wagons, which we emptied hundreds of yards from where we had dug it up. Starting in June 1941, the Germans used this location to hide railroad cars that transported fuel for use in the attack on the Soviet Union. When a German guard clubbed me on the fourth night of this labor I decided to escape. After I had put several dozen miles between myself and Mrozy I met a peasant who agreed to take me to Siedlce in his horsecart. From there I continued on foot and reached home the next morning. When Mother saw me, she danced with such joy that I thought she had gone crazy. When she calmed down, I studied her closely. Although I had been away for only a week, she had aged visibly. I later found out that a young townsman, who managed to run away before me, had told people that none of the workers would make it back home alive.

Before the month was out, Wehrmacht soldiers were posted to Łosice and needed barracks. Many men, including me, were drafted to build the barracks and later to clean them, especially the latrines.

In mid-May the Germans ordered the Judenrat to supply 200 Jewish workers to repave the road to Sarnaki, about 12.5 miles from Łosice and only a few miles from the River Bug. At first we thought the Germans were moving soldiers and supplies up to the Soviet frontier to protect them from bombardments. Each morning, however, more and more soldiers moved in and occupied the finest houses. By the end of May the soldiers had been equipped with many armored vehicles. In June, the streets were so clogged with tanks that one often had to wait hours to cross the road. There was movement around the clock.

On Saturday, June 21, the Germans suddenly left town. We were sure they had gone to take part in an attack on the Soviet Union. If so, bombardments would surely follow. Each family bundled up its belongings. Indeed, the German bombardment began at 4 or 5 the next morning. By 7 A.M., the sky was filled with German aircraft. All the townspeople closed up their homes and fled westward. My parents joined their relatives in Bejdy

We all returned within a week, by which time the Germans had advanced into the Russian interior. I spent the summer working wherever the Judenrat sent me.

Hardly a week passed without a new German directive concerning the Jews. Jews were forbidden to circulate freely. Jews had to remove all metal implements, jewelry, furs, and woolen items from their homes. We were repeatedly fined for alleged infractions of these rules. The worst blow, however, was the establishment of the ghetto, which totally isolated us from normal life.

The Łosice ghetto was set up on December 1, 1941. Since only a small portion of the town was set aside for this purpose, the overcrowding was unbearable. My family had to leave its house, which was outside the designated ghetto limits, and move into one room on Donaj Street. We shared these quarters with a refugee family from Warsaw, meaning that eight people lived in that one room. A family from Ciechocinek, with five daughters, also lived in the building; for lack of choice they occupied a butcher shop. Somebody helped them put up a shelf along the wall in those cramped quarters, to serve as a bed. The place had no heating whatsoever, and the girls had to spend the entire winter on that shelf. Such conditions became routine.

Signs forbidding Jews to leave the ghetto, on pain of death, were posted on every street. Similar notices appeared outside the ghetto, warning the townspeople that the ghetto was infested with typhus and must not be entered.

In fact, a typhus epidemic did break out in the ghetto

during that first severe winter. It claimed many lives, even among young people. The dead were taken for burial in the Jewish cemetery, which was located outside the ghetto, but only one member of the family was allowed to attend the interment.

As an example of the restrictions, the sidewalk on Bielska Street was reserved for Jews but the street for Poles, because it was the main road between the county seat, Siedlce, and Biala Podlaska. Jews were allowed to cross the street at only two places. Sometimes a child or adult forgot this rule and stepped off the sidewalk elsewhere, risking immediate death.

The Germans gave us coupons good for 200 grams (about seven ounces) of bread a day, but the quantity of flour that reached the baker was seldom enough to provide this ration for everyone. Several days after the ghetto was established, a gendarme apprehended three Jews 15 feet outside the ghetto boundary and wrote down their names and addresses. One of the culprits was Miriam Rivka Schwartz. About a week later, all three were removed from their homes at midnight and murdered at the edge of town. From then on, whenever the Germans caught a Jew outside the ghetto without permission they shot him on the spot. On several occasions, my mother wrapped a large kerchief around her head, left the ghetto at 5 A.M., before daybreak, went to nearby villages to barter clothing for food, and returned after nightfall. Chaim Kulewicz, my mother's cousin, was caught outside the ghetto. A gendarme led him straight to the Jewish cemetery and shot him.

The employment of Jews outside the ghetto made it easier for them to buy food. Some artisans whose workshops had been confiscated managed to obtain permits to work outside the ghetto walls. In the ghetto itself, there was no longer any demand for anything except for food. People bartered valuables and tools for bread and potatoes. Many ghetto inhabitants sold everything they owned.

Deportation

In February 1942, the Germans ordered the Judenrat to provide a first batch of workers for the Wolfer and Gobel company, which was going to build the main highway between Siedlce and Brest-Litovsk for the Wehrmacht. This sent the ghetto into a panic, because until then male forced laborers had usually been allowed to come home at night. The only exceptions were a few people who lived in labor camps established in the summer of 1941 for road repair. Even these camps, however, were close enough that the workers could visit their homes at least on Sundays. This time, however, as everyone knew, the Wolfer and Gobel labor camp was located near Siedlce and was tightly sealed. Since some workers from nearby Sarnaki had already been sent to this camp, information about the conditions there was public knowledge. The main type of work, stone-crushing, was especially arduous, and the workday ran from dawn to dusk. The workers slept in unheated barracks and were given scanty rations. One of the names on the Judenrat's list of Wolfer and Gobel laborers was mine.

My parents asked acquaintances on the Judenrat to try to get me exempted, but in vain. Construction on the highway was expected to begin in the spring; even more labor would be needed then. This left me with no options. Weeping bitterly, Mother gave me a bundle with sheets and a blanket. I took a small amount of bread. Mother urged me to take care of myself and gave me a kiss and a hug. Tears welled in my eyes, too, but I tried to keep the other boys from noticing them. I joined the first transport, composed of 207 young Jewish men.

The conditions in the camp were not significantly different from what we had been told. We worked near villages along the Miedzyrzec Podlaski highway, smashing boulders that villagers had collected and hauled to us. The fields were still covered with snow. In addition to all the other hardships, we suffered from the cold and rain. Most of the soldiers guarding us were middle-aged Austrians. Employees of the German firm organized the work, but the overseers were Poles and the group foremen were young Jews who were chosen at random. Those who fell behind or faltered in their work were beaten mercilessly — in several cases, fatally.

A few days after we reached this location, a Pole named Wasilewski was appointed camp manager. He reported to work at 5 A.M. every day, roused all the workers from their barracks, and ordered them to exercise, i.e., to run in a large circle in the muddy yard. Those who could not run fast enough were ordered to lie down on a bench brought over from the barracks and were flogged on their bare backs.

The daily ration was 250 grams of black bread, watery soup for lunch, and chamomile tea in the morning and the evening. For the first few days, the Germans allowed the Judenrat to provide us with extra bread, so each of us also received a half kilo of bread from the ghetto. Families were permitted to send parcels of food or clothing along with the shipment of bread. Some families, however, could not afford such luxuries.

Other workers in the camp came from ghettos in the Mordy, Sarnaki, Sokolów, and Stoczek regions; they, too, received assistance from their local Judenräte. Jews from the Warsaw Ghetto, who composed a large majority of inmates in the camp, had the worst conditions. Since the Warsaw Ghetto had been established much earlier than the ghettos in the small towns, it was the most impoverished. Families there could not afford to buy the extra quota of bread, which meant that the men from Warsaw had to survive on the German company's rations. Most inmates who starved to death — as happened every day — were from Warsaw.

Many workers contracted serious lung diseases and had festering sores. However, the supervisors did not regard these as illnesses and rarely agreed to send a sick inmate home.

By the time I acquired all this information, I had been in the camp for twenty-three days. I was filthy (showering was prohibited), I wore a lice-infested vest, and I had a severe cold and a high fever. Aware that I could not survive in such conditions, I discussed the possibility of escape with my friend, Michael Rak. The next day — it was the seventh day of Passover (April 9, 1942) — we left the camp for work in the pouring rain. The trucks were waiting for us across the road, near a row of small Polish houses. Michael and I stepped into a courtyard and hid behind one of the buildings. After the trucks drove away, we walked across fields until we reached a barn, where we hid until nightfall. Then we double-timed it over the 20-plus miles to Łosice, arriving there before dawn.

My family was delighted to see me. My mother served me a small bowl of soup; I gulped it down and then slept for twenty-four hours straight. When I woke up, I felt much better. Several days later, the Judenrat sent policemen to arrest me and take me back to the camp with a new transport that had been organized in the meantime. When they came looking for me, I hid. Since my father was out working on the main road at the time, they arrested my mother for a few hours. Father, fearing that I would be identified and shot as soon as I reached the camp, contacted the Judenrat and offered to take my place in the transport. When Rak and I had decided to run away from the camp we had not considered the consequences. We had to get away from it and we did so. Only now did I realize how grave an action it had been, and not only from our own standpoint. In the end, however, the Judenrat agents left me alone.

The ghetto was charged with providing workers to build the Siedlce-Brest highway, but this did not exempt the rest of the ghetto population from forced labor in the vicinity. Most residents preferred the latter because, although unpaid, it was easier than road-building.

Men, and later young women, were sent to maintain roads that had been damaged when the winter snows melted, or to repair railroad embankments. During the summer grain harvest, the rural estates needed extra field hands. Sometimes gendarmes patrolling the streets snatched passersby for these duties.

I was sent to the fishponds in Wozniki, an estate about three miles from Łosice. The owner was utterly unmoved by the food shortage and our hunger; all he cared about was that we get our work done. Szczebuński, the Polish overseer, would tell us what to do, leave us alone, and return only to inspect that the work had been done properly.

We came home each evening; that was the best part of the day. Workers on farms farther away from Łosice had to stay there all week. Our duties included cleaning out ponds and ditches that brought water from scum-covered marshes. From time to time we had to drain the ponds and transfer the fish to a different pond so we could clean out the refuse from the bottom.

Winter winds still blew. Evidently I had not fully recovered from my illness, and on Shavuot, in late May, I fell ill again with what Dr. Weitz diagnosed as typhus and pneumonia. I was examined in a building on Swiniarów Street that the Judenrat had set aside for serious typhus cases. I spent three weeks in bed, close to death. There was no medicine whatsoever; even bread was scarce. Mother spent most days and nights sitting at my bedside; were it not for her devoted care, I probably would not have survived. Mother told me later that her three brothers and the neighbors helped her get food for me.

The ghetto became more crowded with each passing day. The nearest town, Sarnaki, was already *Judenrein.* About a thousand Jews from Sarnaki were sent to Łosice and another 500 to Mordy, about ten miles from us. Before 1939, about 5,000 Jews lived in our town. Between ten and fifteen percent of them left with the Red Army when it withdrew to the River Bug in October 1939, but their place was taken by other Jews from nearby villages and western Poland, all the Jews from the town of Blaszki, and escapees from Warsaw. So by the early summer of 1942 the population of the Łosice ghetto had increased to around 8,000.

We began to hear rumors that in German-occupied towns east of the Bug, special SS units were shooting entire Jewish communities. Later on, in the second ghetto, I discovered the source of these rumors. Herschel (Yeheskel) Perlmutter, a young man who had fled to Slonim in 1939 after the Russians left, returned to Łosice and told his relatives that in Slonim a special SS unit had ordered all Jewish men to report to the market square. When they had assembled, they were trucked out of town and shot. Similar things were happening in all other towns in the area, Perlmutter added. We also heard that in Lublin and other nearby towns Jews were being deported from the ghettos for resettlement in unknown destinations. Later we heard that Jews from Warsaw were being treated the same way.

Many of us still believed that the Germans were merely behaving as they had at the start of the war. The conventional wisdom held that the "unknown destination" was somewhere in the Russian hinterland. Nobody knew anything for sure, of course. Nevertheless, we thought we would be spared deportation because we were all working and needed. Still, the possibility of resettlement troubled us as continually and severely as our daily hardships.

After another two weeks at home, I recovered sufficiently to return to the fishponds. I was one of seven laborers there. The work, although by no means easy in midsummer, was not especially onerous. Furthermore, the fresh air helped me make a total convalescence.

One night in early July, several gendarmes entered an apartment near mine and wantonly shot dead one man and two girls. They wounded the other members of the family, who were known as "the Japanese" because of their short stature. The gendarmes ordered the survivors to dig a pit in the courtyard of the building and bury the corpses there.

After this incident, I decided, for safety's sake, to sleep in a stable belonging to my uncle Matis, across from our home. I shared these accommodations with my friend Berl Goldberg, a baker's son; he and his four brothers had formerly lived on the edge of town, on the road to Woźniki. Now his entire household, together with another family, lived in one room on Donaj Street, not far from us.

On Saturday, August 22, we woke up as usual at 5 A.M. to go to work. When we heard gunfire, we became concerned. Since people usually set out for work at that hour, it seemed strange that the streets were deserted. Our house and the stable where we slept were near the edge of the ghetto, with the gendarmerie headquarters and the pharmacy across the street. We peeked over the fence and saw gendarmes passing by now and then.

At a loss as to what to do, we spent half an hour pacing back and forth between the stable and the yard. Suddenly we heard shooting nearby, followed by a woman's screams. I was sure it was my mother's voice. In a panic I raced to the yard and leaped over the fence to see who had been wounded. Across from me, an SS man aimed his rifle at me. I ran behind a corner of the house and immediately heard gunshots behind me. Berl and I rushed back and hid in the stable, afraid that the German would search for me. We lay there quietly, fearing for our families and our lives.

The gunfire intensified. Now it came from the direction of the market square.

We were soon joined by my brother Israel, who had reached us after slipping through a window and crossing the yard unobserved. I asked him about our mother — it was another woman who had been shot, he told me. He added that early that morning the ghetto had been surrounded by SS and SD men, gendarmes, and Polish police. We did not understand what this meant. My brother urged me to go home because Mother was worried about me. We must be together at such a time, he argued.

Just then we heard the Jewish police shouting: everyone, without exception, must come out of their homes and report to the market square. Violators would be summarily shot. Acquainted with the Germans' methods, we knew they meant it. So we went back home, gathered up our clothing, and packed it along with other items we thought essential when being deported to an unknown destination. We stepped into the street, which was swarming with frightened people, each carrying a hastily packed bundle or parcel, tied in a sheet or tablecloth. The residents of the ghetto had already filled the market square. Soon horse-drawn wagons appeared on the scene. Women, children, and old men were ordered to climb aboard along with their belongings, but there was not enough room for everyone. Mother found a place in one of the carts and watched over our parcels.

SS men gave contradictory orders and chaos reigned. Women and children cried. People were milling about. The convoy stopped in front of the church on Siedlecka Street. A gendarmerie officer kicked men and healthy women off the carts and ordered them to line up on the side of the street. Several were shot on the spot.

Some people tried to escape; almost all of them failed. Members of the Goldstein family, owners of the grocery store where I had worked, fled with their tenant, Dr. Sajf, and his daughter in the direction of Swiniarów, but were shot down near the river. Mr. Goldstein was wounded and lost consciousness. Taking him for dead, his assailants left him where he fell.

Dozens of corpses lay on the pavement in the market square, along with bundles and suitcases that were too heavy to haul away. The convoy was ordered to get going again. The wagons carrying children and the ill were the first to set out. They were followed by a long column of people, eight to twelve abreast, stretched back for hundreds of rows. We were sure we were being marched the three miles to the Niemojki railroad station, from which we would be taken by train to Siedlce. We thought that the Germans were going to concentrate all the Jews in the county there. We thought we knew the Germans and their capabilities well. No one had an inkling of the horrible truth.

We marched on, wrapped in a cloud of dust so dense that we could hardly see the way. Some of the guards walked alongside the column; others rode in jeeps on which machine guns had been mounted. The shooting began shortly after we left the town limits. Anyone who straggled was shot at once. Because we walked in such close formation, every bullet struck someone, even if he or she had not been the original target. Those who fell wounded were finished off at once. Even in this terrible distress, people embraced their dear ones and rushed to help one other. I ran alongside my brother and watched over my mother, who was walking behind a cart full of children. Suddenly we heard shots behind us. Everyone hurried ahead.

Later we discovered that during the march the Germans killed hundreds of the elderly, ill, and feeble, including the rabbi of Łosice. People who initially carried their belongings jettisoned them because they had become too heavy.

Although we were dreadfully thirsty, we were not allowed to drink from wells that we passed. It was very hot; dust clogged our nostrils and throats. No one could keep up the pace.

When we reached Mordy, we saw a pile of crushed

suitcases and half-open parcels, all of them empty. We saw corpses, too. We understood that the deportation decree had been applied to the Jews of Mordy, too. We saw abandoned houses that Polish neighbors had already looted of everything movable. We realized that this scene was almost certainly being repeated in Łosice at that very moment.

The procession was finally ordered to halt a short distance from Stock Lacki, several miles from the county seat, Siedlce. The SS officer allowed the carts to move on and lashed out with a riding crop at people who attempted to follow them. He allowed my mother to pass anyway, but when I tried to follow her he struck me in the head and forced me to stay where I was. Tears poured from my eyes as I struggled to make out Mother's retreating figure. I was glad to have taken the blow instead of her. I could not know then that my eyes were following the person dearest to me of all, Mother, for the last time.

We reached Siedlce at twilight. We looked at the wagons that had carried some of the women and children. They were emptied quickly and sent on their way. The peasant carters were allowed to take the parcels and suitcases for themselves. In the streets, Poles were grabbing anything they could pick up, so the wagoners tried to leave town as fast as possible. Everything was open and shameless, as though things like this happened every day.

We were led into the Siedlce ghetto, to the square opposite the burnt synagogue, where the Jewish cemetery had been. Everywhere we saw freshly murdered corpses. There were injured people lying about too, some of them unconscious, others screaming in pain, and others motionless but still breathing, probably no longer able to feel anything.

It was after dark when we moved on, but the shooting did not stop. Since we were too closely packed to pass among the corpses easily, we could not avoid trodding on them. The guards threatened to shoot us; then they ordered us to sit down. I stayed close to my brother. When we sat down they fired over our heads. The screams that followed told us that people were being wounded. Those seated near the victims tried to soothe them — mainly out of fear that the murderers might hear their cries and come back to administer the *coup de grâce*.

During the night, searchlights swept the barbed-wire fences that marked the ghetto boundaries and prevented any attempts at escape. From time to time the German Einsatzgruppe soldiers, General Vlasov's men, the gendarmes, and the SS troops shot into the crowd to sow terror. As we lay on the ground, we whispered our children's and relatives' names to each other, attempting to find out what had become of them. Surely some were no longer alive. Israel and I vainly tried to learn our mother's fate.

When dawn broke the next day, Sunday, August 23, 1942, the German SS soldiers fired intermittently and aimlessly. At about 6 A.M. the Jewish police were ordered to fall out and remove the bodies. They carried them off in pairs — one holding the corpse by its armpits, the other clutching its feet — and loaded them onto the carts. Later, when I returned to Łosice, I encountered a boy of ten or so who had survived the massacre by playing dead.

After the corpses had been removed, the murderers sat themselves down on chairs by the gate and shot at anyone who caught their attention — a woman who wore a hat, a man with a red beard, a girl who wore a colorful dress.... They shot to kill, laughing all the time. Many of those who lay near an intended victim were also hit.

It got hotter as the day progressed, in a repetition of the previous day's weather. As the sun beat down, our thirst increased and became unendurable. It was our second day in a row without water.

In the afternoon we were finally marched off to the railroad platform. The streets were almost deserted; apparently the Germans had taken the trouble to clear them of the locals. To ease our terrible thirst, a few of us picked up mud from puddles alongside the road and stuffed it into their mouths. A bullet soon put an end to their thirst, and their lives. Others raced toward wells in nearby courtyards or into houses; they were cut down by a burst of automatic gunfire. A German who stood near me shot a boy from Łosice in the chest; the wretched child, dripping with blood and oblivious to what he was doing, approached the German and begged him for permission to rinse off the wound. A German officer who overheard the boy's request ordered him to lie down; then he unholstered his sidearm and shot him dead. The only sound to be heard was that of Jews begging the SS guards — water, water, water.

The officer who had killed the boy climbed up on the platform and announced that we would be receiving bread and coffee within a few minutes. An hour later, a fire engine appeared. The mass of people, unable to control themselves, pushed toward the truck from every direction. The firefighters began to spray water on the crowd. People moistened their clothing so they could remove it and squeeze out the water later. Some drank the muddy water that flowed on the platform.

After taking the edge off my thirst in this "shower," I walked up and down the platform looking for Mother, while Israel went to look for her elsewhere. Somebody told us that he had seen her fifteen minutes earlier and that she had asked about us. Although we did not find her, we found my aunt and her children. My aunt told us that her husband Mottl, my mother's brother, had been shot dead in the square in Siedlce.

We were ordered to sit down and stay still. When darkness fell, the nightmare continued. Time and again bullets shrieked overhead, followed by the screams of those whom they struck. We were not allowed to move or to change position. Occasionally someone lost his mind, stood up, and screamed. SS soldiers killed them at once, along with other people as well.

On the morning of August 24 at around 10 A.M. a freight train pulled in and we were ordered to climb aboard. Even as we obeyed, our persecutors screamed at us, shoved us, and struck us with rifle butts. Obviously the SS men wanted the process to go faster. My brother and I were among the first to get on the train; we stationed ourselves near a small vent covered with a grate. However, the car quickly filled up to the point that not only couldn't we move, we even found it difficult to breathe. Some people passed out; only the density of the passengers kept them from falling. Realizing that death was waiting for us, we reacted in the only way possible: we pushed, stepped on people's heads, and with a superhuman effort managed to reach the door. Better to be shot to death on the platform, we figured, than to die of suffocation.

Hundreds of people were still on the platform. The Germans realized that the train was packed to the maximum and attached several more cars. We entered one of them as quickly as possible and shut the door to prevent a recurrence of what had happened before. There were about sixty people in the car, all standing; there was no room to sit.

My aunt, Leah Brukmann, and her three children, Malka, Elta, and Chaim, were also in this car. Soon the train pulled out of the station. It was not long before our thirst again became unbearable. It drove several passengers insane, including an acquaintance of mine from Łosice, Abraham Łosice, a man of about forty. He took off his clothes and began screaming hysterically, impervious to all attempts to calm him.

We had absolutely no idea where they were taking us. We kept hearing shots, single and in bursts, each followed by screams. The gunfire came from soldiers stationed on the roof of the train, who shot at anyone who attempted to escape by leaping from the tiny windows.

Three or four hours later the train finally stopped at a station. Somebody peered out, caught the name of the station, and passed on the word: Treblinka. Some of the passengers recognized this as a stop on the way to Malkinia. We knew that during the past year the Germans had established a punishment camp there, mainly for villagers who did not fill their grain quota for the German army in lieu of tax payments.

We watched people leaping out of other cars, some totally naked and others wearing only trousers. They tottered like drunkards. Too spent to be afraid of the guards, they staggered toward a nearby water pump. Most of them were shot before they reached their destination; others fell as they drew water. A few observed this but, undeterred, tried their luck anyway. To this day I remember the spectacle of Abram Jablonski, a respectable gentleman from Łosice, racing as naked as on the day of his birth. He reached the pump, only to be hit by a bullet the moment he clutched the handle. I thought to myself that he had indeed reached his final rest; the dead are never thirsty. Those who were running toward the pump were only half-aware of what they were doing; their only wish was to moisten their mouths, even if death ensued immediately. I, too, would have sprinted in that direction had I been sure they would let me drink before I died.

Suddenly I noticed, about a dozen yards from our train, a women of thirty or so, dressed only in pants. She approached the SS officer and pointed to her bosom. It was clear that she was asking him to shoot her. The officer struck her several times with his riding crop, but she held her ground, again pointing to her breast. The officer, evidently losing his patience, stepped aside, called over one of the soldiers, and ordered him to shoot her. She straightened up and turned her head toward this junior murderer. After the loud report of the gunshot, her legs buckled and she sank to the ground. I admired her courage.

About twenty of the sixty cars in which we had arrived were uncoupled and left at the station. Only then did we realize that we had reached our final destination. The camp must be nearby, we reckoned. We were impossibly thirsty and did not know what would become of us. People from other cars continued to jump onto the platform, desperate for water. Later I found out that most of the people in the overloaded cars had died of dehydration.

Even in these conditions, however, money and especially jewelry were of value. Poles who worked at the station approached an SS soldier and asked for permission to distribute water to the thirsty people, and he agreed. They carried buckets of water over to the cars and filled the bottles that passengers pushed at them. But they charged dearly for each bottle. Polish money was not good; they would accept only hard foreign currency or valuables such as rings, earrings, and brooches. Without them you could not get water. These "compassionate" Poles evidently split the proceeds with the soldiers. Somebody in our car gave them several gold coins, for which we received a genuine treasure: a small pail of water. Unfortunately, by this time no one was behaving rationally; as people jostled to get closer to the bucket it tipped over. As a result, no one got to drink, not even the person who had paid for the water. Only those right next to the puddle managed to lap up a bit of water from the sodden floor.

Treblinka

The locomotive came back and towed away twenty more cars. Our car stayed where it was. I sat down in a corner and fell asleep; night had begun to fall. I awoke to the sound of my brother's sobbing. Everyone around us was sobbing. A few people prayed; mainly I heard *Shema Israel.* Others embraced their loved ones and bid them goodbye. A few, in their despair, pounded their heads against the walls of the car. I pushed my way toward the small peephole and looked out. All along the platform, corpses were heaped up. We couldn't see any farther, because a long building blocked our view. Nothing was moving. Although at the time I didn't know anything about the gas chambers and the crematoria, I was sure we had been brought here to play our part in the Nazi genocide scheme. We all believed that the soldiers were going to shoot us the minute they opened the doors of the cattle cars. Several minutes later, when the doors were opened, we were struck by the sickening stench of burning flesh. The German and Ukrainian guards bellowed at us to hurry up. Those who did not move quickly enough were beaten with rifle butts. Some of us got out of the cars but could hardly stand on our feet. Others sank to the ground. An order was given: men and older boys to the right, women, children, and the elderly to the left. My brother and I joined the right-hand column. We gazed at the left-hand column as it disappeared through a large gate. I was puzzled about why so few people were coming out of the cars. Soon I found out why.

We were ordered to remove from the train those who had suffocated or who lay motionless. In every car there were corpses, lying in every conceivable posture. In some cases, entire families had died together — mothers still clutched their children, husbands still embraced their wives, mouths still agape, as if gasping for air. Sometimes three generations lay together in a befouled corner. I knew some of the dead; they all came from my town.

I found my cousin Esther Yocheved, with her three red-headed daughters and her husband, all dead. Before the war, they had lived in Wloclawek. Lying nearby were my uncle Matis, his wife, and his daughter, married only a year earlier.

In pairs we carried each corpse out to the platform, where the pile rose to a height exceeding that of the tallest man. Some of the dead still frothed at the mouth, a sign that they had perished within the past few hours. Others still showed signs of life: although unconscious, they wiggled an arm or leg. Some groaned, perhaps for the last time. The corpses, as well as those still wavering between life and death, were taken to pits that other Jews had already dug. I heard Germans shouting "*Arbeiten, arbeiten,*" and Ukrainians shouting, "*Raboti, raboti, bo bodu strelt*" — "Work, work, or I'll shoot." Although we had never heard Ukrainian before, we understood perfectly, because it closely resembles Polish.

Heaped up next to the pile of corpses was a vast pyramid of parcels, bundles, suitcases, and clothing — the belongings of victims who had arrived on earlier transports. My brother and I occasionally hid under the pile of rags to rest, but not for long, because the guards ordered us to get out and go back to work. Despite everything, we still wanted to live. We were still afraid of death.

We worked all night under the searchlights. Many people who started working with us died before the night was over and were taken away exactly as they had dragged off other bodies. Only luck determined who lived and who died. Israel and I toiled doggedly until daybreak. Early that morning, a bulldozer appeared and began to excavate three large, deep pits near the fence. Later the locomotive came by, pulling three flatcars. About twenty-five Ukrainians and Germans were standing on the first and third cars. Twenty prisoners, including my brother and me, were ordered to climb aboard the unoccupied middle car. We were each given a small cup of lukewarm water, not nearly enough to slake our thirst.

The guards opened the gate and we left the camp. The Ukrainians told us that we would not be coming back there; we were going to work in the forests. Soon we found ourselves at the Treblinka railroad station. Dozens of corpses were strewn on the platform and along the tracks — evidently persons murdered the previous day. Amidst shouting and blows of rifle butts we were ordered to load the corpses onto the flatcar. We worked on the run, without a moment's rest. Those who could not run or who moved too slowly were beaten with rifle butts. Later, two guards ordered me and three boys to follow them. We climbed down from the platform and walked toward some dense vegetation. On our way, we had to cross a shallow stream. Unable to control ourselves any longer, we sank to our knees and drank deep drafts until the guards aimed their rifles straight at us.

Across the stream we saw two bodies, apparently those of would-be escapees who had managed to make it that far before being shot down. One of them, a middle-aged man, was still clutching a handful of banknotes; others were strewn around him. He had evidently tried to buy off his murderer, but the bribe was not accepted this time. Whoever caught him had no trouble taking his money and the valuables in his pouch, and killing him too. One of us recognized him; it was Nissim Rosenbaum, a well-to-do Warsaw merchant who was born in Łosice and had returned to his hometown along with his family when the war began. We lugged the two corpses to the car and loaded them aboard.

In addition to the bodies there were severed legs, arms, hands, and other body parts lying between the railroad tracks. We were ordered to load them aboard the flatcars, too.

After we finished our work we were led back to the camp. After we unloaded the bodies, we joined the other workers. Later I figured out the source of the dismembered bodies: people who had jumped from the train and hid under the cars but were too exhausted to go any further. When the train pulled out, they fell and were crushed under its wheels.

After we returned to the camp, an SS man appeared, accompanied by two young men carrying pails of water. Quickly we lined up and waited to drink. However, the German saw something he didn't like. He unholstered his gun and suddenly I found myself prostrate on the ground. I felt no pain but realized that I had been shot. As if in a dream, I heard somebody lying next to me sobbing and mourning his father's death. I was weak but still conscious. The right side of my white shirt was stained with blood.

I lay there as the column advanced slowly. Suddenly I heard somebody saying, "He's still moving. Maybe we should ask the SS man to finish him off; why should he suffer?" Apparently somebody was concerned about me. I agreed with him. This terrible camp was no place for the healthy, let alone for the wounded. Either way, my time was numbered. Within seconds, however, my brother was next to me. The moment he saw me he burst into tears. I told him to stop crying; this was no place for tears. All of this happened next to the platform and the hut filled with piles of clothing stripped from the dead. Israel and somebody else dragged me over to the hut and lay me under a pile of clothes.

I asked Israel to find a towel so I could clean out the wound. He removed my blood-stained shirt and wrapped me in a towel that the workers found nearby. Then he dressed me in a shirt that was too big for me, so the towel fit inside. It turned out that the bullet had penetrated my chest on the right side and exited from my back. Israel concealed me in a stack of clothes and went out to look for water.

After I drank the water he brought me, my pain got worse. I wanted to find an SS man and ask him to put an end to my agony, but Israel began to cry again and pleaded with me to reconsider. He had just lost his mother; he didn't know if his father was still alive; and now I, too, wanted to abandon him. That was more than he could bear; if I died, he too would no longer wish to live. He had to survive, I told him. He was the only member of our family who could avenge our deaths after the Germans lost the war. My luck had run out; he still had a chance. He was young and healthy and had to carry on.

My brother sat down next to the place where I was lying under a pile of rags. Then, to avoid attracting attention, he started working with the young men who were opening and sorting the orphaned parcels. I raised my head and gazed into the cloudless blue sky. I could not recall if I had ever noticed its beauty. Suddenly, I recovered my will to live.

The parcel-openers found a bottle of iodine in one of the packages and gave it to my brother, who poured it into my wound. It stung horribly but I was determined to prevent infection. I hoped the wound would eventually heal. Somebody found a sugar cube and gave it to me to suck on. The pain erupted again — this time it was so severe that I ripped off the towel that served as a bandage. Just then my cousin Chaim Brukmann peeked in. He told Israel that

Dr. Majes was hiding in the long hut and might be able to help me. The two of them gripped me under the armpits and dragged me around the corner, into the hut. Dr. Majes was no longer there. He was a young doctor from Lwow who had served with the Polish army at the beginning of the war and been taken prisoner. Freed in 1940 but unable to return home, he had settled in Łosice.

The hut was stuffed to the rafters with parcels and bundles bearing the names and addresses of people from Radom. We found several people there whom the doctor had helped. One of them, well concealed among the clothes, was a friend of mine, Julke Goldberg; he had been shot in the elbow. I decided to share his hiding place. Israel arranged a comfortable spot for me among the piles of rags. My whole body was covered, except for my face, and he stacked several bundles on my left side so I could hide my face, too, if necessary (my right arm was totally disabled). Then he went out to look for water. I never saw him again. I do not know and never will know what became of him and how he perished. He may have been hit by a stray bullet, as I had been. It made no difference to the murderers, for whom we were just a herd of slaves doomed to extermination in any event.

Several moments later I heard one of the guards shout, "Get out, get out, or I'll shoot." Within seconds I covered myself totally. I knew I could not obey the order even if I wanted to. The guard climbed on the heap of parcels. At one point his foot came down right over my head. He discovered a few concealed men and I heard him shoot them dead. I think I must have lost consciousness.

It was not yet evening when I woke up to the sound of machine-gun fire outside the hut. Breathing heavily, I pressed my wound with my left hand and obtained a little relief. Soon afterwards, my friend Julke Goldberg crawled toward me and told me that his brother, Sane, was lying dead next to us. He, too, had gone out to look for water and had been spotted by the guard on his way back. The guard followed him in and killed him with the others. In the same breath, Julke told me that he had dreamed that he and I would survive.

His dream strengthened my resolve to stay alive. I wanted to believe him. Unfortunately, only part of the dream came true. Several days later, Julke joined the ranks of the dead.

The next morning, August 26, I crawled out of my hideout and saw three young men drinking. Half-dead with thirst, I asked them to share the water with me. One of them replied that they were drinking urine, not water. I pointed to my chest, told them that I had been shot and could not go outside, and was very thirsty. One of the men poured a little of the cloudy liquid into a cup, measuring it as if it were a rare treasure, and gave it to me. I sipped a little but it did not quench my thirst.

On Thursday, August 27, I heard from the men in the hut that a transport had arrived from Miedzyrzec Podlask. A transport from Kielce had also come in during the day. Before sunset, a young man clutching a pair of scissors approached me and asked me to cut his long hair. Unable to move my right arm, I could not do as he asked. Instead, I asked him to search through the parcels, hoping that he would find something for me to drink. He found a small bottle of vinegar and poured a little of it onto a sugar cube. I popped the cube into my mouth. My lips, tongue, and gums stung; it was vinegar concentrate. Nevertheless, it gave me some relief because the burning helped slake my agonizing thirst.

The boy also tasted a drop but refused to drink more and gave me back the bottle. I put it in the pocket of my trousers. About half an hour later, I felt a strong burning sensation in my thighs. Slipping my hand into the pocket, I found the bottle empty. The pain was unbearable. Fate had played an especially cruel trick on me, I thought. My back, too, ached and itched, because it was still peeling from sunburn that I had incurred before the deportation. My back had blistered on the way to Treblinka and was now covered with scabs. I was uncomfortable no matter how I lay. But worst of all was the thirst.

On Friday, peering through the cracks in the walls of the hut, I noticed that water was being doled out next to one of the large pits near the fence. Barefoot, and taking care to remain unnoticed, I stepped out of the hut and swiftly mingled with the group of workers. Now it took four men to drag away one body, each holding an arm or a leg. The corpses had become heavy and bloated, swollen to approximately twice their natural size. Their skin was deformed by insect bites; their clothes seemed to be covered with grease. These people had suffocated aboard the train and their bodies had been lying next to the platform for days. The workers had to get used to the stench of the decomposing flesh. I wanted to join the corpse-draggers to get a little water but was roundly rejected. I didn't look like someone who could help. Indeed, I more closely resembled the dead who were being tossed into the pit. I understood the workers' concern: I might attract the murderers' attention. Finally I found a three-man team that agreed to accept me as its fourth member. Each time we brought a body to the pit, we received a little water. From time to time soldiers fired in the air to expedite the work. On one occasion I took advantage of the commotion to slip back into the hut and bring Julke some water.

The next day, August 29, marked a week since I had left Łosice. That morning, I heard men at work near the main entrance to our hut, and discovered they were nailing it shut. I realized that we had to abandon the refuge; if we stayed there, we would die of thirst. Julke was afraid to leave because the bandage on his elbow was visible, so he stayed anyway.

When I left the hut, my first thought was to look for my brother. I hoped he was still among the living. I looked around, scouting for someone whom I knew. My eyes fell on Gedalia Rosenzweig, my friend from *cheder* and the son of Shaya the builder. My appearance had changed so severely that Gedalia did not recognize me; I had to tell him who I was. He told me that only seven people from the Łosice transport were still alive and led me to them. All had been assigned to clothes-sorting duty and wore a red patch on their pants. Unfortunately, none of them knew what had become of my brother. Two of the seven had been hiding with me in the barracks: Jakob Müller of

Wlodzimierz (in Volhynia) and Michael Fischmann, a relative of the Goldstein family, from Biala Podlaska. They told me that three days earlier the Germans had selected fifty men for labor and then murdered all the others.

All the clothes-sorters had been given a red triangle that they sewed or attached with a safety pin to their right trouser leg. They called the *Gruppenführer* — the group leader — a heavy, solid man, *Wiener Fleischer* ("the Viennese butcher"). I think his real name was Singer. As a special gesture they had not killed his wife. Gedalia found a piece of red cloth among the rags and attached it to my pants with a safety pin. Before sunset I reached the enclosed barracks area where the "legal" or "special" workers were supposed to assemble. An SS man came over and began the roll call. He counted us and found too many people. Holding the list in his hand, the man walked back and forth, looking for the culprit. When he asked me my name, I answered, "Gedalia Rosenzweig." He located the name on the list and moved on. He came across another suspect and asked him his name, too — but before he received an answer he was called away. Seizing the opportunity, I went into the barracks and concealed myself under the rags that the workers had brought previously. The *Gruppenführer* completed the roll call. When the workers entered, I sighed with relief; I was still alive. But no one could know for how long. We lived not only from day to day but from minute to minute. The pain in my right side and arm had become unbearable.

That night I lay in the dirt alongside Gedalia. I could not

fall asleep, because on the hard ground I was unable to find a comfortable position that could ease my agonies. My whole body ached; every posture was torture. At most I managed to doze off briefly.

At sunrise we were sent out to work. We worked in a large field behind the building where I was hiding, where the clothing and parcels were stored. A mountain of bundles rose about two hundred yards to our left. Three hundred yards to our right, just inside the fence, there were three deep pits where they burned the corpses. About 650 yards straight ahead was a chain-link fence; beyond it were the gas chambers. With my left hand I lay coats, dresses, and underwear on a sheet that had been spread out. When it was full Gedalia tied the corners into a bundle and took it over to the stack.

The other workers were nearly finished with the job of clearing all the corpses from the platform. Some of the bodies had lain there for ten days and were in an advanced state of decomposition. Armed guards patrolled among us. SS men kept showing up to pick a few of us out of the rest and lead them to the edge of the huge cremation pit. There the victims were ordered to disrobe and stand facing the pit. Then they were shot to death. At first, each of the victims had to drag the body of his predecessor into the pit; his reward, when he climbed out, was a bullet. Anyone who pleaded for his life was ordered to lie on the ground and absorbed a terrible beating before being shot. Most of these people, however, had become too indifferent to ask for mercy, knowing that that virtue had lapsed from the world. Brutal and untrammeled murder had become so routine that any German or Ukrainian might kill at any time. I do not remember a single case in which a person selected at random in this fashion was allowed to live for even a short while.

Several days passed without transports. The workers cleaned the platform, covered it with burned-out coal, and laid fresh branches along the fence. But the stench of charred corpses hung in the air. In the barracks at night we bolstered one another's morale, trying to construe the changes as an indication that the ordeal was about to end and our release was imminent. The older workers cited the absence of transports and the clean-up work ordered by the SS men as evidence that a Red Cross team from Switzerland would soon visit to investigate the camp. Some went further and asserted that Allied aircraft were bombing German cities because the Germans were murdering innocent people. We wanted to believe that the world was reacting to the mass murder in some fashion. These prophecies definitely strengthened our resolve. Others did not share our optimism, though; several of these realists hanged themselves each night. Workers hauled their bodies away in the morning.

During my stay in Treblinka, we ate mainly what we could salvage from the victims — bread, sausage, and sometimes delicacies that we had not seen in years. Some deportees believed they were being taken to a camp where they could live together with their families; they brought their best clothes, food, money, and valuables. Thus, although we were always short of water, the incoming transports kept us from being hungry. We were not allowed to eat during work hours because the food that the deportees had brought with them was the property of the Third Reich. The usual penalty for putting something in your mouth was death.

One day, five SS officers who were not part of the regular camp detachment paid Treblinka a visit. They were accompanied by an officer from Treblinka whom we had nicknamed "Lalka," Polish for "doll." He evidently gave them a tour of the death factory. Several minutes later, as we busied ourselves sorting clothes, two guards came up and selected me and other members of the group, forty in all. One of the guards ordered us to stand on the side and form a column. As the men complied, I slipped away and rejoined those who had not been selected. I still do not know what prompted me to do that. The forty selectees were led toward the pits. About fifty yards from the last pit, the guards told them to undress. Six of them were ordered to go over to the pit, where the SS men were waiting, and stand facing it. At Lalka's order, they were shot in the back of the neck. Then each gunman kicked his victim into the pit. The next group of six were led to the same fate. The slaughter continued until the last victim had been murdered. None of them asked for mercy.

The young German whom we called Lalka was an especially handsome and elegant man — always nattily dressed, clean-shaven, boots gleaming. No one would ever have guessed what kind of beast lurked behind the handsome facade. To this day I cannot understand how people who must have had normal parents, homes, wives, and children, who went to school and who believed in

God, could carry out such atrocities and return home after their day's "work" to eat dinner, go to sleep, and perform all their other daily activities. Nor can I understand why we still wanted to live. My thoughts, like those of an animal, focused on one thing only: finding a way out of this trap.

Every day we worked until sunset, followed by roll call, which included the workers with the red patches. Roll call was conducted in an area between the barracks where the workers slept and the hut where the new arrivals undressed. The Germans did not have a list of workers' names; a head count was enough for them. I understood that after each day's shootings they wanted to know only how many workers would be available for the next day's labor. After roll call, we received a little hot water and some half-cooked potatoes. That was our supper.

I think that by this time the number of red-patch workers toiling under the command of the "Wiener Fleischer" had grown to between sixty and eighty. We were privileged to have a separate entrance to the large barracks, where a wall separated us from the rest of the prisoners. In the absence of a floor, 200-250 workers slept on the sand in a larger area of the same barracks.

One evening, aircraft passed over the camp and the staff immediately turned off the searchlights. Our morale soared. We believed that Russian bombers had arrived to destroy the death factory and hoped that at least some of us would escape and tell the world what was happening there. Unfortunately, nothing came of it. Several minutes after the aircraft passed overhead, we heard dull reverberations of bombs, but far away — perhaps near Malkinia. Later we consoled ourselves with the knowledge that the Germans must have suffered serious damage.

The next day, when we went back to our cleaning duties, we found a sign with a seven-paragraph message. One paragraph spoke of showering and delousing; another was about sorting clothing and tying pairs of shoes together by their laces. Money, valuables, and documents were to be stuffed inside. Later I learned that before victims entered the "showers" they threw off their clothes where they stood, leading to a situation of tens of thousands of unpaired shoes. The Germans, with their innate thriftiness, had to put some order into this chaos. The Fatherland could not tolerate the wasting of resources that were now state property.

One evening, the SS men divided us into labor details. Together with Gedalia Rosenzweig I was sent to join a forty-man crew. Each of us received a broom. Working in pairs, we cleaned out railroad cars after their passengers had been removed. Now we knew why the Germans had made us fix up the platform: to dupe their new victims into believing that they were about to be interned in a labor camp. All the rumors about international committees were no more than wishful thinking.

The first new transport arrived the very next day. Twenty cars, each guarded by an SS man, stopped alongside the platform. The train carried people from Warsaw, who still looked relatively healthy and certainly were in better condition than those in the transport from Łosice. The weather had cooled off; the cars were less crowded. The Germans prodded the passengers to exit the cattle cars quickly. As they rushed to comply, the workers cleaned up after them. All the men, women, and children were quickly pushed into a hut, where they were ordered to disrobe; from there they were led directly to the gas chambers. The empty railroad cars were towed out of the station. As soon as all the newcomers had finished undressing, the Germans prodded the workers to remove their clothing, parcels, and shoes as quickly as possible and carry them to a spot behind the long hut. A short time later a locomotive arrived, pulling another twenty cars. We repeated the process for the rest of the transport.

New transports stopped at the platform the next day, but by now we were more sophisticated. The moment each train stopped, we went into action and handed our brooms to some of the new arrivals. The brooms proved that they were workers, and we, in turn, were protected by the red patches on our clothing. The newcomers swept out the cars and we removed the trash from the train and dumped it into the burning pit. Afterwards, the newcomers mixed with the veteran workers and returned the brooms. At roll call, our murderers could not distinguish between "legal" and "illegal" laborers. In their frustration, the guards shot many people from both groups.

In retrospect, I don't think the Germans cared about our ruse one way or the other. Certain that we would all die in the end, it was all the same to them who dragged out the bodies and who sorted the clothing. They spared those among the newcomers who said they were construction workers, because at that time they were building new facilities to improve the slaughterhouse and make it more efficient.

We also heard that the Germans spared pretty women, whom they kept around for gang rape by German officers and Ukrainians, and then murdered them. Only men were employed in the parts of Treblinka where I worked. Once someone called my attention to a young woman dressed as a teenage boy, who was sorting the clothes with us. I don't know how long she survived.

When each transport arrived, the women were always the first who were ordered to take off their clothes. Lalka strolled alongside them and, after they stood naked, whipped those who were ashamed of their nudity or covered their private parts with a sheet or a piece of cloth. Sometimes he lashed one of them simply to inflict pain.

By now the transports were coming every day. One day was much like the next; the same incidents recurred again and again. Once, as I swept out the interior of a car, an SS man suddenly struck me with his whip and ordered me to help a woman, who was unable to stand, climb out of the car. The idea was to show his victims how well the ill were being treated. Then he ordered one of the workers to take the woman to the field hospital for care.

The newcomers really believed that the ailing woman would be taken to an infirmary. None of them realized that the "field hospital" was in fact just a giant pit, about thirty yards in diameter, which was always ablaze. They would place those who were sick or disabled on the ground at the edge of the pit, facing in. The SS man in charge circulated among them and shot them in the back of the neck; then the workers cast them into the pit. Some of the victims were still breathing when they were tossed in with the other bodies.

The pit was separated from the spacious field by a barrier of fresh pine branches, which were replaced from time to time to conceal the "infirmary" from the newcomers until the last moment. Twenty minutes after I helped the woman climb out of the railroad car I was told that some infants were sitting by the pit, and no one else was there because the SS soldier had taken his lunch break. I gathered some trash and went over there. I saw the woman whom I had removed from the car, still breathing, sitting at the edge of the pit and staring in fright into the burning inferno and its contents: the half-cremated bodies of old people and children, mixed with smoldering trash. She tried to stand up, but her legs would not hold her. She looked at the workers who stirred the embers — remnants of human beings — so they would burn better. Nearby were about a dozen infants, too young to have learned how to walk. They were not crying — they certainly did not understand what was happening. They looked about, almost certainly in hopes of finding their mother or father. Later I heard that right after he returned from his lunch break the SS man shot them all and ordered the workers to throw the tiny bodies into the flames. Of all my memories of that accursed place, the vision of these babies is undoubtedly the worst. I see their faces whenever I remember Treblinka. As I write these lines, more than fifty years after that day, I still cannot overcome the horror.

The atrocities mounted in number with each passing

day. Every evening I was surprised to find myself alive. Members of our work detail vanished every day. Once forty or fifty Jews passed through the gate, half-dead, and were driven like cattle toward the gas chambers. Some of us believed that they had been marched to Treblinka from a nearby labor camp. Whenever prisoners were sent to the gas chambers, replacements were selected immediately; but they, too, survived only until they had deteriorated to the condition of their predecessors.

One day, all red patches were ordered inside the barracks. Everyone else — at least 300 men — was ordered to undress and dispatched to the gas chambers. I was afraid that an SS man would come to recheck the names and discover my identity. Just then, however, a new transport came in. Some of its passengers were selected to join us, which messed up the count even more. The grapevine had it that the Germans "replaced" us so frequently because they had heard that we were planning an uprising.

The next day, some of us, including me, were ordered to join a group that was earmarked for extermination. They told us to go to the barracks and undress. By this time I had enough experience to know that obedience meant death. As before, I was determined not to die now. Behind the barracks where we slept, workers were digging a new pit to serve as a latrine. I decided to join the group. An armed Ukrainian guard stopped me, shouting *"kuda?"* — "Where?" — and tried to block my path. I stood up straight and without hesitation answered that I had been sent to work here. He pointed his rifle at me but, even though I was gripped with dread, I kept striding forward until the other workers could see me. An acquaintance of mine who worked there, Jakob Müller, spotted me and began to shout at me to get back to work. Grumbling, the Ukrainian allowed me to move on. Others, wishing like me to survive, tried the same thing. I went to work right away; many of the others perished before the day was out.

A new transport from Warsaw came in on September 7. Again I had to sweep out the cars. A seasoned veteran by this time, I immediately handed the broom to someone else. Later, in the square, the new sweepers would join those who transferred and sorted the possessions. We called them "Lumpenporters." Those who came with us to collect valuables from suitcases were called *Goldjuden* — "jewelers."

One of the workers was a young Warsaw Jew whose nickname was "the Gypsy." He was no more than twenty when he arrived, driving a horse cart. His job was to ransack the victims' suitcases and collect delicacies such as cocoa, canned food, cheese, and dried sausage for the Germans to eat. Once, when the Gypsy spotted a worker secreting a piece of candy in his clothes, he jumped down from the cart and demanded that he put it back. The worker, a newcomer in Treblinka, saw no reason to obey the orders of another Jew, even one who held an official position. The Gypsy began hitting him with his riding whip but the worker, undeterred, pushed the Gypsy against a wall. Suddenly three SS soldiers appeared. When the Gypsy complained to them they only mocked him. At this, the Gypsy, the murderers' lackey, struck and killed the helpless Jew. The SS men looked on in equanimity; afterwards, they ordered the Gypsy to send two men to carry the body to the burning pit.

I found the episode disgusting. I could not banish the idea that we should kill the Gypsy. We all wanted to survive, but not at the expense of others. Indeed, every time we passed on our brooms to newcomers we reduced our own prospects of survival — but we took the risk anyway. I discussed the episode with the members of the group and made a request: "If anyone finds a knife in one of those suitcases, bring it to me." I planned to corner the Gypsy in the area where he gathered his booty. It would have been easier to kill him in his sleep, but he did not live with us.

The next evening, the roll call found 200 extra workers, even though there had been many murders that day. This was due to our broom-sharing and various other ruses. The SS men ordered the "illegals" to identify themselves. About sixty men stepped forward. After a few moments the SS men ordered all of us to go to sleep. The next morning, they held another roll call; again the 200 extra men were ordered to identify themselves and the same sixty people obeyed. The Germans chose another 140 men at random and led them off to the gas chambers. Jakob Müller was one of them.

That day I heard that the German kitchen supervisor had shot the Gypsy dead after discovering that the latter was hiding money. In Treblinka, death was the penalty for such a crime — in fact, for any infraction imaginable. Any Jew who could still breathe was ipso facto a criminal, and all the more so one who broke the rules. A member of the labor detail told me that he had seen the German kitchen superintendent lead the Gypsy to the pit and shoot him at its edge. I was pleased to hear this, although I would have preferred that he meet his death at the hands of one of us.

That afternoon, we were ordered for the first time to load bundles of victims' belongings onto the empty trains. We knew that the goods were going to be shipped to the central warehouse in Warsaw, or perhaps to Germany. Several times I tried to enter a car and hide under the suitcases, but the loaders working in the train did not let me in. Before they locked each car, the Germans checked to make sure no one was hiding inside. Had they caught a stowaway, they would have held the loaders responsible. But when the second group of cars came, I found two husky teenagers from Łosice working in it. I remember only one of them; his name was Leizer Mordski. Everyone else was hauling bundles. The suspense was so great that I forgot the pain in my right arm. Michael Fischmann passed me a belt filled with gold coins, which he had previously concealed in the sand near the platform. When the car was partially filled, I carried a bundle inside. But instead of going back out, I hid in a corner near the window. When the car filled up halfway, Michael Fischmann and Gedalia climbed in and joined me under the bundles. Michael was the oldest of us, about twenty-four. Evidently anticipating our future needs, he had concealed several belts filled with gold coins that he had taken from corpses.

We lay there, anxious and tense, sweating from the heat

and the lack of air but mainly from fear. In the meantime, our comrades added more bundles to the car until there was no room left. When they finished, Leizer Mordski called the SS men to come over and inspect it. We held our breath as the German soldier rummaged through the bundles, until he said "*in Ordnung*" — "Everything's okay" — and jumped onto the platform. Some time later, we heard the heavy door being slammed shut and locked. We lay in total darkness for about half an hour more until the locomotive lurched into action and the cars began to move. I climbed up a bit and peered through the slats of the grate. The platform began to fade into the distance. Several shots were fired, but they were far away. Suddenly I realized that I was outside. I had escaped from Treblinka. At that moment I could think of nothing else, not even the unknown destination of the transport, not even whether we would manage to get out of the car before the Germans opened it.

I think we left the death factory on the afternoon of Wednesday, September 9. I had been there for seventeen days, each of which was more like a century. It would be more appropriate to reckon the time I spent in this inferno in seconds, not days.

Leizer Mordski, who had helped us escape, was the son of the owner of an olive curing plant. He had lived with his family on Miedzyrzecka Street in Łosice. He managed to escape from Treblinka the same way we had. In early July 1944, when he was in the Konstantinów area with two additional comrades, soldiers of the Polish nationalist "People's Army" (the Armia Krajowa) killed him. The

Red Army liberated the area only three weeks later.

I later found out that Jakob Müller of Wlodzimierz (Volhynia) had managed to elude death after I saw him being led away with 199 additional victims. He survived in Treblinka for almost a year. In August 1943 he took part in the uprising and escaped from the camp. Until the liberation, he hid in the forests along the River Bug. We met again after the liberation. Today, he lives in Montevideo, Uruguay.

After the war I learned details about the German camp staff. The commandant when I was there was SS *Obersturmführer* Imfried Eberl, a respectable physician in civilian life. Lalka, the "doll," was a certain Kurt Hubert Franz. He came from Thuringia, where he had worked as a waiter. When we were in the camp we assumed that the Germans had recruited our tormentors from among criminals or deviants. But it seems that the Nazi regime had the power and allure to attract ordinary people, too, to commit the most unspeakable acts.

Later, I discovered in Gitta Sereny's book *Into That Darkness* that, at approximately the time I arrived in Treblinka, Franz Stangl came from Sobibór to take over the command of this factory of death. He was the commandant of Treblinka until the prisoners' uprising in August 1943.

Escape

Instead of accelerating, the train inched along and stopped at the Treblinka station. We heard people running and shouting. Suddenly the car began to rock and we realized that we had not been discovered, but that the train was simply being switched to another track. We also felt additional cars being hitched up to the train and assumed that these, too, were carrying victims' clothing. Enveloped in total darkness, we could not know whether we were within earshot of the Nazis. I felt a sense of suffocation, not only because I was covered with rags but also because I had to cough. I suppressed my coughs as best I could to avoid attracting attention.

Around midnight, the bolt on the door of the car was pulled back and we heard several men conversing in Polish. I was frightened: they must have heard me coughing and were searching for us. We heard the doors of others cars being opened as well. About an hour later, the silence resumed. After seventeen days of hearing the murderers' incessant gunfire and their victims' terrified screams, this silence filled us with dread. Where was the train going? In what direction? Would we find a way to jump off it?

Around 5 A.M. the train began to move again. When we were certain that the Treblinka station was several miles behind us we crawled out from under the mountain of clothing in which we had been buried.

At the top of our agenda was the need to find out which way our train was headed. We surmised that it was probably going toward Malkinia, from where it would continue to Ostroleka or Warsaw... or maybe to Siedlce. We prayed for the latter option, of course, because that would take us closer to familiar surroundings.

When a beam of light penetrated the car we realized that the door was not locked. Looking around, we discovered that some of the bundles had been removed while the car was standing in the Treblinka station. From this we inferred that the inhabitants of Treblinka and the vicinity had opened the door to exploit the new economic opportunities created by the Germans' monstrous schemes. I approached the door and peered out carefully. The train was moving along an embankment that traversed a flat and muddy area covered with low vegetation. Farther away, on the horizon, I could make out a green forest and, here and there, the silhouette of an isolated house. Unfortunately, I could not figure out where we were or what direction we were headed in.

The train continued moving slowly; at least, that was how it felt to us. Subconsciously, we may have thought that the farther we got from Treblinka, the safer we would be. Gedalia suggested that we jump off the train. No one was around, he argued, and we could choose the appropriate time and place. Such a convenient opportunity might not come our way again, he said. Michael and I objected: we were still near Treblinka and had no doubt that railroad guards were patrolling the area. The more distance we put between ourselves and the slaughterhouse, the safer we would be, we thought. Furthermore, we didn't know where we were.

The train began to slow. We must be approaching a station. Quickly we buried ourselves under the pile of clothing, but closer to the small window this time. When we pulled into the station, I slipped out from the clothing and read the sign: Kosow Lacki. This meant that were near Sokolów and, more important, heading toward Siedlce. Fortune was smiling on us, we felt. Perhaps we would beat the odds, even though they were stacked so heavily against us, and survive after all.

When the train stopped, our car was a short distance past the station. Through a crack, I watched two men walking alongside the train. One of them called the unlocked door to his comrade's attention. They reached into the car, removed several bundles of clothing, and took them to the other side of the train. They repeated this action many times. Their pilfering did not overly concern us. To our misfortune, however, when they were done they slammed the bolt shut and locked the door of the car. Evidently the Germans had serious rivals for the property they had looted. By the time the train reached Warsaw or Germany, we thought, it would be almost empty. We conjectured that the unplanned stops were arranged by the train crew and inferred from this that there was no guard on the train. Since we were now locked in, though, our only escape route was through the small window. It would be very hard to squeeze through this opening, and doing so would make it more dangerous to jump from the moving train.

Soon the train began to roll again. It passed several small stations without stopping. Then the locomotive whistled; we thought the train would stop at any moment. Through the window we saw a sign — Sokolów Podlaski — but we passed this station without slowing. We knew that the next station was a small one several miles past Sokolów. Through the window we saw railroad workers tossing coal out of the tender. We knew that the engineers padded their scanty salaries that way. During the occupation, everyone made off with whatever could be moved and saw nothing wrong with that. Indeed, stealing from the German occupiers was considered commendable. From the standpoint of the locals the contents of our train were assuredly German property.

The train lurched forward again several minutes later, but slowed to a crawl after covering about a mile and a half. Men opened the doors of the cars, removed bundles of clothing, and tossed them to the ground. The three of us seized the opportunity and jumped out the small window. As we ran toward a nearby orchard we were intercepted by a tall young man who was clutching a huge bundle under his arm. He approached, stopped, and smiled amiably. "You've escaped from Treblinka, haven't you?" Then, without waiting for an answer, he added, "I'll show you the way to town." We guessed that he was referring to Sokolów.

Fischmann, the oldest of us, said, "Thank you very much, but it's better for us to hide in the forest during the day and wait until dark."

The young man agreed at once. "Right. I'll help you find a place to hide. But first I have to get rid of this bundle. Wait for me; I'll be back in a moment," he said.

Fischmann, pleased, brandished a wad of banknotes and stuffed a 100-zloty note into the man's hand. This brought a sudden glint to his eyes. "Don't be so stingy!" he said. Fischmann gave him more bills. We realized that Michael had made a terrible mistake when he showed the young man that we had so much money. The Pole hurried away. Before we could consult with each other and decide what to do, the stranger returned with another man and demanded payment up front. Fischmann gave them all the money that the first man had seen, plus a diamond ring and additional valuables. They pocketed it all and told us to stay put. After they stowed all their bundles they would come back to help us find a hiding place.

We did not trust them. As soon as they moved out of sight we dashed into the forest. After fleeing for about half an hour we came upon an elderly peasant who was grazing his cows. He saw at once that we were Jews and warned us not to enter Sokolów. Earlier that day, he said, SS platoons and companies of Lithuanian militia had moved toward Sokolów.

Two of Gedalia's brothers were working for Wolfer and Göbel in the camp on Brzeska Street in Siedlce. One of them spent every day smashing boulders in neighboring Mokobody. Would it be possible for us to join those workers and then return with them to the camp in Siedlce? And might my father still be alive? Together we could cope with all these terrible hardships! Stubbornly I backed Gedalia's idea. Mokobody was straight ahead.

The friendly peasant explained how to avoid encountering what he called "the force" by using side roads. He told us that Mokobody was about ten miles from Sokołów; to reach our destination we would have to go through Sikory, Świniary, and other small villages. We knew, of course, that our route would really be longer because we had to detour around all these places. We set out after devising a plausible story to tell anyone we might meet on the way: We were laborers for Wolfer and Göbel and a German driver had delivered us to the Przewozki area to collect rocks from the fields. The driver went off and had failed to return to pick us up. To avoid unpleasantness, we were making our way back to Mokobody and expected to be taken to Siedlce with the rest of the workers.

Near one of the villages, we passed an old woman who was grazing her cows. Although she asked no questions, I told her the story and asked for help. She pointed the way. We did this repeatedly, fine-tuning the story each time until we began to believe it ourselves. Our route took us across forests and fields and around villages. We filed along narrow paths and forded innumerable muddy creeks. After we passed Świniary, the steeple of the Mokobody church hove into sight. My anxiety mounted;

now we would find out whether any Jews were working there. I was especially afraid of what I would discover when I asked whether my father was still in the camp.

We reached the vicinity of Mokobody at roughly 5 in the afternoon. To ease our hunger and thirst, we decided to try our luck at an isolated cottage. The woman, however, would not let us draw water from the well in the yard and called her husband. A tall young peasant, wearing high boots, materialized from behind a corner of the cottage, carrying an infant in his arms. He asked who we were and what we were doing there. After we told our story, he burst into laughter. "I've never seen Jews from a camp dressed as well as you are," he said. "You must have jumped out of a train going to Treblinka and are carrying lots of cash and gold!"

After appraising the tip of the gold mechanical pencil that protruded from Gedalia's coat, he snatched and examined it and put it in his pocket. He grabbed the gold watch on my wrist. Then he took hold of my coat and ordered me to remove it. Finally, he demanded money. I wrenched the coat from his hands and shouted that he should choke on everything he had already taken from us. Then we hurried on, not stopping even to drink.

We had better luck a little later. We reached a tiny hut that was home to an elderly childless widow. She gave us water but had no food at all. She offered to go to her neighbors and borrow a little bread from them. Since she had made a favorable impression on us, we decided to wait. About fifteen minutes later she returned, clutching a warm loaf of bread, which — not having eaten in more than twenty-four hours — we consumed at once.

Later she told us how to use side streets to reach the market square, where Jewish prisoners were working. We paid her well, even though she had not helped us out of greed. Her magnanimity toward us bolstered our morale and reinforced our belief that there were still generous people in the world.

A spacious area in the market square had been set aside as a workplace for Jews. This area was piled with boulders and stones brought in from the vicinity. Exhausted men in tattered clothing smashed the stones into gravel for building roads. The pieces of stones formed small geometric patterns. At one edge of the square was a latrine knocked together from boards and sheetmetal, evidently built by the Jews and meant for their use. We decided to hide there from the Germans and the Polish overseers. We were not concerned about the Jewish foremen.

We sneaked in and found the place empty. We knew that the Germans allowed workers to use the latrine only at fixed times. Soon, when the workday was over, the workers would rush in. To prevent a crowd from forming around us we decided to keep mum about Treblinka and our escape from there. Instead, we concocted a new story: we had escaped from the transport about three weeks ago and reached Sokolów. When we heard that some people from Łosice were still alive and had been sent to the camp on Brzeska Street and that some prisoners from the camp were working in Mokobody, we decided to join them. The Judenrat in Sokolów had helped us and even given us 500 zlotys apiece.

The sudden silence after sunset indicated that the day's labors were over. Several men entered the latrine building. Noticing us at once, they began to ask us questions. Where had we come from? Why did we come here? We recognized several of them as being from Łosice. They told me that my father was fit and well, working as a gardener for the German camp staff. They had heard about Treblinka but were unable to sift truth from falsehood amidst the swirl of rumors about gas chambers, murder, and the cremation of human beings. They still deluded themselves that the survivors of the death march might be alive in some distant location, perhaps in Belorussia (White Russia) in the Soviet Union.

Workers kept coming up to us and asking whether we had news of their wives and children. The younger ones asked about their parents and other relatives. Perhaps we had seen them? If not, had we heard anything about their fate? Everyone knew about the deportation, the death march, and the murders that had occurred on the way to Siedlce, but no one had lost all hope. They thought the deportees had been sent somewhere and were still alive. Finally, several flatbed wagons hauled by tractors pulled up. We merged into the group with no difficulty and climbed aboard with the others.

It was totally dark by the time we reached the camp where I had spent the early spring. As soon as we jumped off the wagons the workers began to form up into groups. A head count took place, but things were so chaotic that it proved easy to deceive the Germans. I was led to my father. I find it difficult to describe the reunion that followed.

Father cried like a little boy. I wanted to cry, too — tears of joy at having found him at long last. But no tears would come. I told Father that Mother and Israel were dead, as were all our relatives from Łosice. Almost all the other inmates had already lost their loved ones, including their immediate families. I told him the entire terrible story, leaving out nothing, but asked him not to share the information with anyone. I learned that a small ghetto still existed in Siedlce, with about 2,000 people, almost all of them men still able to work. Łosice also had a tiny ghetto, much smaller than that in Siedlce, occupied mainly by Jewish policemen who had been spared from the deportation, along with a few other survivors. Their living conditions were apparently tolerable.

That evening, I lay next to Father on his bed of planks. Although exhausted, I could not fall asleep. We talked and talked. My father's eyes were swollen with tears. Finally, I slept briefly, until I was rudely awakened by Menachem Zilberstein, a Jewish policeman whom I had known back in Łosice. Zilberstein was angry that I hadn't told him I had been in Treblinka. Gedalia or Michael must have incautiously confided in someone and the story spread like wildfire. Menachem suspected that I was concealing the truth about his family. In fact, I knew nothing about their fate. I denied that I had ever been in Treblinka. Perhaps Gedalia or Michael had been there, I said, but I had gone no farther than Sokolów. Zilberstein let me be, but I knew we were on thin ice.

In the morning, Menachem came back with orders: I was to report to Moshe Hubermann, a Jew from Lodz who had recently reappeared in the camp. Hubermann was on friendly terms with the camp commander, Wasilewski, and commanded the Jewish police in the camp. Known as an informer and an extortionist, he harassed anyone from whom he thought he could squeeze a little money. Michael and I went to him. Hubermann said he heard we had been in Treblinka and possessed a great deal of money. He demanded 200 zlotys from each of us for what he called the "general fund." We denied we had been in Treblinka and told him that we had long since spent the money we had received in Sokolów. But I volunteered to sell my good pants and Fischmann offered to sell his jacket, and we promised to give him the proceeds if he let us stay in the camp. I argued that he knew very well that we had nowhere else to go. In the meantime, as a good-will gesture, we gave him our "last" fifty zlotys as a down payment. Fortunately for us, he did not know how much more money we had. Although we accepted his terms, we had no doubt that his appetite would grow over time.

This incident showed us that we could still expect many difficulties and that this camp would be only the first stop on our escape. We had to decide when to leave and where to head. Most of the ghettos in the district and beyond had already been liquidated, we knew. Those of Węgrow and Sokolów were exceptions, but their proximity to Treblinka left little doubt about their eventual fate. There were several labor camps nearby, but we had heard that working conditions there were extremely harsh. Conditions in the small ghetto in Siedlce were even worse than in our camp. People were picked up and tortured to death every day and the congestion was so severe that many of the residents had nowhere to sleep. By contrast, in what remained of the Łosice ghetto, women cleaned houses and men worked on the roads or helped renovate the new gendarmerie headquarters. We hoped we could be reunited with friends and, perhaps, find some relatives alive. We might even find trustworthy Poles there, we speculated. Above all, we really had no choice. We decided to run away from the camp that evening and walk back to our hometown. Father promised to join us later but for the time being preferred to stay in the camp.

Ours was the largest camp for Jews in the vicinity. It had about 2,000 inmates, including 200 Gypsies who worked in separate squads and received better food than ours, because according to Nazi ideology they were members of a slightly less-inferior race. Only trusties and the infirm spent the day in the camp. "Infirm" meant too weak to walk. For such prisoners, death was only a matter of time. They lived in a room where bodies were piled for several days before being transferred to a mass grave. All the camp inmates suffered from malnutrition. The German firm provided only the minimum daily ration needed to sustain life: 250 grams of bread, often moldy, and a small portion of watery soup. Black-market bread was expensive; after the deportation few could afford it. The main job was maintaining the highway between Siedlce and Miedzyrzec Podlask. During the day, enterprising prisoners often pilfered produce from the field or solicited handouts in the villages.

On this particular day, after Hubermann left, we

discovered that our labor detail had already gone out for the day. I spoke with several prisoners. Most of them had lost their will to live when their wives and children died. Only the youngest inmates still spoke of escape. Thinking about Father, I realized that he had recovered his will to live only after seeing what I had gone through. Evidently your will to live depends on having somebody who needs you. Father was about fifty-six at the time.

We tried to lie low for the rest of the day. We hid under the rags that covered our plank beds and tried to get some sleep. We were in dire need of rest, because that night we were planning to walk the twenty miles to the small ghetto in Łosice.

The camp was ringed by a high double fence, with soldiers manning watchtowers at the corners. Sometimes, though, the searchlights went dark. Father showed me the holes in the fence through which one could crawl.

At twilight, Father and I embraced at length. I gave him some of my money and valuables to help him survive. The escape proved quite simple. We figured out when the labor details would pass through the main gate on their way back. While they drew the guards' attention, as we knew they would, we slipped through the fence and crawled across the potato fields beyond it until we were far enough from the camp to stand up without being seen. Soon we reached the Siedlce-Niemojki railroad line. We felt that the rails were safer than the road, where we might encounter the village guards. So we walked through the dark along the old line to Mordy, which traversed unpopulated marshland and bypassed the villages on the way. Our only fear was that we would bump into the German railroad guards.

As we walked along the embankment in the pitch dark, we spoke in whispers, with occasional stops to make sure that no one was walking ahead of us. It was a warm night. The moonlight picked out the low scrub that covered the marshes, occasional clumps of trees, and now and then a glimmering pond. We kept our eyes straight ahead, afraid to blunder into the railroad guards. After walking several miles we assumed that we were nearing Stock Lacki. Shortly before the bridge over the Liwiec River we climbed down from the embankment, in case there were guards on the bridge. We trod through hundreds of yards of swamp water, channels, and rivulets, detoured around the bridge at a safe distance, and returned to the embankment. When a freight train approached from the direction of Siedlce we hid in the bushes until it passed. As we neared the Mordy railroad station, we again left the embankment so as to steer clear of the guards. Just short of Wojnów we veered away from the tracks and followed the road to Łosice. We walked single file on the side of the road, ready to jump into the ditch or hide behind a bush if we saw anyone approaching. Cars passed us twice but we managed to hide in time.

We did not dare enter the town by the main road, the bridge to Siedlecka Street. Instead, we followed a stream toward a grove of trees where we had been fond of playing as children — the place we had called the "orchard." Crossing a narrow path, we came to Kiliński Street. Before the deportation, it had been part of the ghetto. Now the area looked like a killing field after an epidemic. The streets were strewn with rags, papers, shattered furniture, and feathers from down comforters. Many windows had been stripped of their shutters; others had been relieved of their glass. We were too scared to absorb this. We knew that we were near Szajewizna, the small ghetto, a reserve inhabited by a few people whom the masters of the Third Reich had chosen to protect — the handful of survivors who had thus far managed to avoid the fate of their fellow Jews.

The Small Ghetto

Szajewizna and Kiliński streets ran parallel to each other. The second ghetto, where the Jewish survivors lived, occupied the area between the market square and Narutowicza Street. The ghetto consisted of three two-story buildings and several one-story frame-and-stucco buildings. After the round-up on Saturday and Sunday, August 22-23, any Jews caught hiding were shot on the spot. That Monday night, however, the authorities in Siedlce ordered the members of the Sonderdienst (the "Special Service") to transfer any Jew they found to the lockup next to the town hall. Two days later, the detainees were taken to a new ghetto, which was already populated by young Jewish women who had been brought in from farms in the vicinity. Jewish policemen, who had been separated from the masses in the courtyard of the old synagogue in Siedlce before the deportation, were also sent back to this ghetto to join the young women — but now to serve as unskilled laborers.

During the roundup, several families refused to assemble at the market square as ordered. More than thirty people went into hiding on the second story of a building on Miedzyrzecka Street, abutting the market square. Some of them were captured the next day and shot to death; the others were taken to the small ghetto. Among them were the Pinkus, Łosice, and Mordkowicz families. Almost all the survivors were young unmarried men or orphans.

Several inhabitants of the ghetto contacted Polish acquaintances and asked for help. The fortunate few received assistance for a time; the rest were turned away empty-handed. The Germans had announced that anyone caught providing aid to "the lazy and criminal Jews," or even speaking with them, was subject to grave penalties, along with their families. Nevertheless, rumors about the existence of a refuge for the accursed began to spread in the countryside. Gradually the escapees heard them and began to trickle into the Łosice ghetto. Often escapees came there in the hope of finding some scrap of information about the fate of loved ones; others did so to stock up on clothing and blankets before fleeing again. A few came to extract valuables from the family safe, so they would be able to pay for a hiding place.

There was an unwritten rule that anyone who came to the ghetto received temporary shelter and a warm meal. Sometimes the refugees were lucky enough to encounter a friend of their parents. After such an experience, few wished to resume wandering the countryside in search of a hideout. They stayed because they felt safer with Jews and because experience had taught them that extortionists would hound them wherever they went outside the ghetto.

Escapees on the way to Treblinka made their way to the

Łosice ghetto — mainly teenage boys and a few teenage girls. On the way back they had hidden in the fields and raided gardens at night, sleeping in furrows, hay ricks, or isolated barns, protected by the warm summer nights. Aware that they were fair game for anyone, they avoided the towns and passersby. The younger ones still hoped that in Łosice they would encounter a friend, a distant relative, a childhood buddy, a friend of their parents, or any friendly person, if only for one last time. All were eager to bond with someone. None, however, forgot the brutality that he or she had experienced during the roundup and deportation; they too had heard the rumors that all the deportees had eventually been murdered. Some were convinced that everyone was doomed; others merely suspected that the fate of the new ghetto would be no better than that of the previous one. For this reason, many lived from one day to the next.

Ironically, and as a result of the tragic circumstances, the lot of some of these survivors improved temporarily. Some men who had not managed to support their families in the old days now found it rather easy to live on their own. They could move into an abandoned apartment, find some valuables, and have enough to eat for the first time in years. Orphan girls returned from the farms at loose ends. Hence it was not astonishing that bizarre romances developed between couples years apart in age or so different from each other that they would never have become intimate in normal circumstances.

Before this large influx of returnees, living conditions were better than they had been before the deportation.

People relocated to apartments or individual rooms on a "first come, first served" basis. When conditions worsened later on, people began to share dwellings with relatives, acquaintances, or other newcomers. The erstwhile policemen took over an apartment that had belonged to Moshe Goldstein. Artisans were ordered to establish workshops and received orders from well-connected Germans and Poles. Machines, tools, and raw materials were hauled in from the deserted large ghetto or provided by the customers. Although the customers did not pay the artisans for their work, they sometimes gave them material compensation if they were pleased. Tailors, shoemakers, and cobblers needed comfortable rooms where they could receive Polish policemen, their wives, and mistresses, who came to be measured.

Several dozen people, mainly women, were chosen to empty out the old ghetto. This meant collecting and sorting the belongings that had been left behind in the abandoned houses. Each category — berets, hats, trousers, coats, houseware, bedding, furniture — was stored separately. Some people who had been selected for this duty managed to get around the authorities and appropriate something for themselves. Occasionally they found something of real value. In general they were allowed to keep any food they found in abandoned apartments.

A large detail was assigned the job of repairing the building past the dairy on the main road to Niemojki. The idea was to renovate the building, formerly the property of Dr. Wroblewski, to serve as gendarmerie headquarters.

The workers were ordered to strip the tombstones from the adjacent Jewish cemetery and use them to erect a fence around the building. The fence still stands. Many inmates found work in the service of the gendarmerie, the Arbeitsamt (labor office), and other German institutions. At times they were forced to spend hours or days at odd jobs. Others were still mobilized for the road-building project.

The deportation of the Jews of Łosice solved an additional problem: overcrowding in Polish towns. Congestion rose steadily after the start of the war because hundreds of families were deported from western Poland. The Germans were generous when it came to giving away the Jews' abandoned homes. The first to receive them were white-collar workers, collaborators, and anyone who had personal connections with Germans. As a rule, the new owners exploited Jews to clean their dwellings — without remuneration, of course. Afterwards, they scoured the ghetto for furnace repairmen, painters, and carpenters who could handle miscellaneous repairs. Although they were not paid for their labor, the Jews were pleased to have these jobs, which allowed them to leave the ghetto during the day and sometimes even for a whole night. This clearly enhanced personal security. The employers were aware of this fact and exploited it. They pointed at the object in need of repair or overhaul, told the Jews what materials to use, and that was that; the Jewish workers had to procure the materials at their own expense. The Poles believed that all Jews were rich and that by employing them in this fashion they were actually doing them a favor.

Not everyone had work, however. Those who could not work or could not obtain work spent their days hiding in the ghetto, which was risky. Occasionally gendarmes raided the ghetto in search of workers. They beat up the first Jews they encountered and then dragged them off to work at the gendarmerie headquarters.

A new elite took shape, composed mainly of former policemen, most of whom were young men from well-to-do families. They were the first to move into the best apartments. They still had their parents' money, retrieved from the family strongboxes. Living for the moment, they often got together to drink and gamble at cards. Most of those who returned to the ghetto lacked the means to live that way; they were continually preoccupied with obtaining enough food to survive. Others who still had money did not flaunt it, because that kind of behavior was dangerous. Anonymous informers frequently denounced persons with concealed funds to the Polish police. Sometimes the hoarders got off with a beating; in other cases they were locked up until they paid a ransom.

The barbed wire that surrounded the new ghetto was largely symbolic. Officially, the death penalty was still in effect for anyone caught outside the ghetto. During the three months that the small ghetto survived, the Germans seldom invoked it, however. Every excursion from the ghetto was risky, of course, but most persons caught on the outside got away with the excuse that their assigned workplace was nearby. This relative freedom of movement made it possible to buy food and other goods from the Poles. Money, too, was more available at this time, mainly because those who were "cleaning" the old ghetto brought back whatever they could to sell later. People were even dressed better, because they could appropriate the best clothing of those who had perished. We few survivors owed our unexpected relative well-being to our murdered brethren.

When we reached the "Jewish island" it had a population of about 200. We were allocated a tiny room, an unexpected luxury for us. We were the first to reveal the truth about Treblinka. Although stories about the death camp had reached the ghetto before we arrived, they were widely rejected as vicious rumors. People clung stubbornly to the delusion that the deportees' fate was not so dismal. Some turned to us in hopes of hearing news of their families. They considered themselves duty-bound to collect every scrap of information about their dear ones. Most of the time we could not answer their questions.

People advised us to find regular work as quickly as possible. I soon found employment on the highway. The overseers were Poles and the working conditions not especially harsh. We made a deal with the guards: in return for a daily bottle of vodka they did not keep strict tabs on us when there were no Germans around. We still had to fill our quota, though. My detail went out as a group each morning and returned in that fashion every evening. Sometimes we could do business during working hours or rendezvous with a peasant to buy food from him. I coped with the situation rather well.

On several occasions the ex-policemen invited me to join them for a drink, but I refused. They simply refused to think about the future. Often it seemed to me that the small ghetto was totally unreal and that I was living in an insane asylum. After Treblinka, the place seemed like a mirage that might vanish in a second. Ever since I had arrived, reason told me that the Germans would not have established a slaughterhouse on the scale of Treblinka while allowing other Jews to stay alive. I discussed this idea with other people in the ghetto. They all admitted that I was right but no one knew what to do. Neither did I. When my comrades and I had fled Treblinka we were driven by only one thought: to "go home," even though we knew that the home was no longer ours. We did not expect to find a place where we could live legally. It was merely that instincts prompted us to return to a familiar location. That was our only goal. Now, having attained the goal, we understood that it could only be a temporary solution. We had not ensured our survival, but only a moment of respite, which we had to make the best use of.

Many inhabitants of the small ghetto, especially men who were alone, refused to think about the next step. Some had found a woman to share their lives. Unwilling to believe the cruel fate that awaited them, they hoped that matters would eventually work themselves out. The air was full of rumors similar to those we had heard in Treblinka. The International Committee of the Red Cross had intervened in Berlin, people whispered. The Allies were threatening to take sanctions against German prisoners of war. The Foreign Ministry in Berlin opposed the mass murder because it complicated Germany's relations with the neutral countries. According to the arguments I heard each day, every additional murder was contrary to the Germans' best interests. We had access to newspapers, but the reports from the front seldom raised our morale. At that time, the Germans were fighting for Stalingrad and advancing toward the Caucasus. We prayed that they would be defeated and retreat in humiliation. Perhaps that would lead to revolt in Germany. World War I had ended just that way, the older men related.

Some time later, the Germans began selling off abandoned Jewish property. Reports spread like wildfire in all the villages in the area. First they sold clothing. People from Biernaty, Skolimów, Hotycze, Swiniarów, and nearby villages came to Łosice in the early morning and formed a queue that snaked for hundreds of yards. Some spent the previous night in town to assure themselves a good spot in the next day's line. No one knew in advance what would be sold on a given day, but this didn't really matter. There were sales every few days. Although the dates were never advertised in advance, somehow the Poles always knew when to show up.

The first objects sold were berets and hats. A few days later it was the turn of shirts, trousers, undergarments, bedding, and other items. Each time the Germans removed the best merchandise before making the rest available. Preference was given to privileged Poles who worked in German offices, Polish policemen and their families, and anyone they liked. Those who were especially privileged sometimes got what they wanted for free. But everyone else, too, paid low prices. Occasionally the shoppers got into fights. The proceeds were supposed to flow into the state coffers, but no receipts were given.

Soon after all the clothing and furniture had been sold off, the authorities decided to tear down selected buildings in the old ghetto — old, ramshackle structures and buildings in inconvenient places such as the market square. The buildings earmarked for demolition were auctioned off. The prices were low anyhow, but the buyers had a special incentive: they hoped to find valuables that the Jews had hidden in furnaces or walls. Stories in this vein circulated later, but were seldom true, because even in the best of times wealthy Jews had not lived in these houses.

Soon after the deportation, the gendarmes announced that the large ghetto was off-limits. Anyone found there without permission would be shot. The Germans wanted to prevent looting, since they considered any abandoned belongings to be Reich property. However, the inhabitants of the small ghetto, who worked in teams to "clean" dwellings in the old ghetto, had been pilfering long before that. After I arrived in the small ghetto, several people were murdered for attempting to steal confiscated property that had already been placed in storage. One of them was the local chimney sweep. The workers told me that they had seen his body in the furniture warehouse, the skull smashed in, lying in a pool of blood on a mattress that he had stolen. He had no luck. After spending all his life sleeping on a straw mattress, he had just stolen what for him was a "luxury" and slept on it for the first time.

One day the gendarmes brought Yitzhak Meir Rosenzweig, the octogenarian father of the chairman of the Judenrat, to the ghetto. On the day of the roundup, the old man decided he would rather die in the place where he had spent his entire life than be hauled off to an unknown destination. He went into hiding in a loft that he had previously used for storage. He stocked enough water and food for a lengthy stay, as well as poison to swallow when these ran out. He disappeared for a month, spending his time in solitary prayer, oblivious to what was happening around him. Then some young men hunting for hidden "treasure," and assuming that something had been left in the loft, broke down the wall and found Rosenzweig there. In a panic, the old man rushed back to his old apartment and shouted for the police from the balcony. It had not occurred to him that now a policeman was much more dangerous than a burglar. The gendarmes came, confiscated his property, and took him to the small ghetto. Like the rest of his generation, Rosenzweig was a religious Jew. He spent his last days in perpetual prayer, along with another old man named Bezi, who had avoided deportation by hiding in his home. The neighbors fed him until the ghetto was liquidated. Then the two old men put on their *tefillin* and prayer shawls and walked to their final destination.

We took the fact that the Germans allowed Rosenzweig to live in the small ghetto as proof that they wanted to deceive us. Relatively gentle treatment of Jews, in this stage, had to be a ruse to persuade us of their good intentions. The Germans knew that many Jews were still hiding in the fields, vacillating about the advisability of seeking shelter in the ghetto. They also knew that some ghetto residents were planning to escape. Many of us realized that the ghetto was a trap that would eventually be slammed shut. It was just a matter of time. We only hoped that we could escape before it was too late. Many others surrendered to a sense of fatalism; others had nowhere to run.

Around that time my father returned from the camp. All his belongings had been stolen there and he had no idea who the thief was. The culprit may have assumed that I had left some money with him. Perhaps he was one of the prisoners who had been in the same barracks; then again, he may have been a Jewish policeman in cahoots with the camp commander. The loss was severe, since every penny could help us survive. In such horrible times, however, these were trivial concerns. Our reunion was an invaluable boost to our morale.

It was also around then that an incident occurred that could easily have ended in disaster. One evening, Polish police suddenly surrounded our building. The commander entered the Jewish policemen's apartment, where I happened to be. I noticed that three names were written on his pack of cigarettes, so I gave a fictitious name. Fischmann gave his real name and was led away, along with his brother. As soon as I could, I fled and hid in a sawmill. The policemen took the Fischmanns to the Jewish cemetery and searched them, but found nothing. Then they beat them and ordered them to reveal where they had stashed the silver and gold they had brought from Treblinka. After torturing and threatening to kill them, the policemen transferred them to the jail. The next day, I sent Yankl Łosice, who was acquainted with the police commander, 5,000 zlotys to forward to him. Obviously someone had squealed that the three of us had escaped from Treblinka and had money in our bags.

About five weeks after the deportation, Miriam Perlmutter, whom I had known since childhood, materialized in the ghetto, along with her sister. The story was that Miriam and her family had gone to the market square on the day of the deportation. Only her brother Hershik, who preferred to go into hiding, wasn't there. Miriam and her older sister walked all the way to Siedlce. When they reached Stara Wieś, a suburb of Siedlce, they decided to take advantage of the darkness to escape. At the last moment, however, they stopped to say goodbye to their parents. At that moment, somebody seized their arms from behind. Turning around, they saw an SS man. In their fear, they attempted to break free. But he wouldn't let go, told them to be calm, and pleaded with them to trust him. Miriam's sister asked him where the people were being taken. He answered by waving his hand at the stars. Still clutching their arms, the SS man led them to a side street where there were neither Jews nor passersby. He told them not to return to the ghetto under any circumstances, because the Jews there were about to be killed. Since Miriam's features were not obviously Jewish, he suggested that she come to the Gestapo building in Siedlce the next day and ask for the chief cook. He would provide her and her sister with Polish papers so they could survive.

The next day, as she was on the way to Siedlce, she met someone who knew she was Jewish and warned her that the Germans were patrolling the streets and killing any suspected Jew on the spot. Panic-stricken, she retraced her steps. After five weeks in hiding, the two sisters returned to the ghetto. Their case was exceptional — it was the first time I had heard of a German disobeying orders. Germans of conscience still existed after all.

It must have been in the middle of October 1942 when a young woman arrived in the small ghetto, clutching an infant in her arms. Memories arose of seeing those babies on the edge of the pit in Treblinka, and I cried uncontrollably for hours. It was the first time I was able to shed tears since the day of the roundup.

With each passing day, more and more people began to look for ways to escape. However, they discussed it in general terms only. Details, especially about isolated locations that could be used, were kept strictly secret and divulged only to those expected to join in the break. A few people contacted Polish acquaintances in town or in the villages for assistance. Only after the liberation did I find out how others had managed to survive.

After the war, I discovered that there had been organizations that helped Jews, but they operated only in Warsaw and not in our vicinity. I never heard of a single case in which the Catholic Church helped a Jew. At that time there were no organized underground resistance groups in our area. Farther away, in the forests around the River Bug, Russian prisoners of war had managed to escape from the camps, but defenseless people like us were easy prey for bandits.

Villagers who agreed to shelter Jews demanded huge

sums of money, less for their personal needs than in compensation for the risk involved. Their peril was real. No one doubted the severity of the punishment that would be visited on peasants and their families should the Germans discover that they were harboring Jews. They had to be even warier of their neighbors than of the occupiers. In the circumstances, everyone was a potential enemy. The price of a hideout varied from place to place but was usually denominated in gold rubles or dollars. Few could afford it. When we left Treblinka with the gold-filled belts, my share came to 140 gold dollars and 220 gold rubles. I saved as much of this money as I could for my eventual safe haven.

Anyone who looked "Aryan" and could speak Polish without an accent tried to buy Polish identity documents. In addition to the price — 3,000 zlotys — acquiring them required connections with somebody reliable in the town hall. To the best of my knowledge, only women availed themselves of this route. Several people survived by posing as Poles and getting themselves shipped off to Germany as laborers. Others headed for Warsaw, where they soon perished. Not a single male of my acquaintance acquired Polish papers. They were pretty much useless for men anyway, since they could not conceal the evidence of their circumcision.

Miriam furnished herself with Polish documents. I helped by donating fifteen gold rubles to the cause. Unfortunately, she did not survive the war; I never found out how she died. After the liberation, I heard about several women from the small ghetto who managed to survive on Polish papers that allowed them to work in Germany: Chaya Goldfader, Bracha Silberberg (whose family once lived on the market square), and Bracha's aunt, Friedl Rosenbaum.

In the first years of the war, many affluent Jews handed over their belongings to Poles whom they deemed to be reliable. They believed that these Poles would guard their belongings and valuables until the end of the war. Indeed, some of their heirs in the ghetto got in touch with these Poles and asked for their property back. Most of the "custodians" sent them packing, maintaining that their parents had already reclaimed the property or denying that they had ever received anything for safekeeping. Some even threatened to call the gendarmes. Everyone knew that Jews had no legal protection and could not sue them. We were all doomed, they figured, and Poles could not be forced to honor agreements that they had made with Jews.

Destitute escapees sought shelter in the fields or forests. They gathered whatever food and clothing they could and hoped to outlast the war — which they believed would not last more than another six months. Some attempted to acquire weapons, but in vain. A few moved into bunkers long before the small ghetto was liquidated. They included Hershik, Miriam's brother, who eventually perished along with the other people who shared his refuge.

Father and I hoped to have some forewarning about the liquidation of the ghetto. We listened to rumors attentively, scoured the newspapers, and made sure to read between the lines. In early November, we found an official advertisement that affected us in the *Nowy Kurier Warszawski* ("New Warsaw Daily"): as of December 1, all Jews in the Warsaw district would be restricted to six designated urban quarters. The names of the six towns were listed; one was Siedlce. The notice took the ghetto by storm. Everyone talked about it; but, as always, opinion was divided. Optimists interpreted it as a good-will gesture on the part of the Germans, who, they fantasized, wanted to concentrate the Jews in specific locations for use as labor. No other interpretation of the notice of the creation of a new ghetto was logical, they argued. If the Germans were planning to kill us, the optimists maintained, couldn't they simply surround us wherever we were now and ship us right off to Treblinka?

Others argued that the very appearance of such a notice in the Polish press was highly suspicious. A Jew confined to a ghetto or a camp was not the master of his fate. The Germans had him under their thumb; if they wanted to transfer him to Siedlce or Warsaw, they hardly needed to give him prior notice. They could simply make the decision and move him that very day. No good-will gesture was needed, and the Germans had never made such gestures to the weak anyway. The idea behind the notice, the pessimists maintained, was to seduce Jews who were hiding out in the countryside. In their despair, they might give credence to the advertisement. The pessimists all agreed that the stipulated date, December 1, should be considered as marking the beginning of the liquidation. We might be transferred to Siedlce first, but the next destination was undoubtedly Treblinka. It would be much more difficult to go underground in the unfamiliar neighborhood of Siedlce than here, so those determined to survive had to vanish before the end of the current month.

Several days later, the papers carried fascinating reports, this time about the situation on one of the fronts. It seemed that the Axis armies were swiftly retreating in Egypt. American and British forces were driving the Germans out of northern Africa. Although pleased by this news, we all understood that these victories were too far away to affect our liberation in the foreseeable future.

In the coming days, people began to disappear, sometimes several at a time. Control over the ghetto population was sloppy. The gendarmes conducted occasional head counts but could not verify the presence of anyone in particular because they did not have a list of residents' names. When a person who worked outside the ghetto decided to vanish, someone else who entered the ghetto took his place. Escapees from other camps and towns kept replenishing the population. Everyone realized that the safest thing was to find a regular job. But with winter approaching, work in the fields would soon end. Farmers and German overseers began to shed unneeded laborers. It was not especially hard to leave the ghetto. The problem was finding a safe haven — and getting there.

Father and I began looking for a peasant who would hide us. Father had grown up in the countryside and always kept in touch with villagers, except when he was in the army. Even so, the search was not easy. No one we contacted was willing to take the risk, for any sum. Nor did we know how long we would have to stay concealed.

Noah, my uncle's brother-in-law, suggested that we hide together in a bunker and take along my cousin Yankl, who was still in the Siedlce camp. Noah told us that he had connections with a peasant in Zakrze, a village two miles from Łosice, who would certainly let us hide on his farm. We immediately accepted his offer; that very evening Noah and I set out for Zakrze to negotiate with the peasant, and, if possible, to begin digging a bunker at once. We walked up Sokolówska Street as far as the cemetery, where we had to cross the River Toczna, a tributary of the Bug. As we forded the stream, Noah slipped and one of his legs sank into the water. After we had advanced several hundred yards he suddenly changed his mind. He must have been a very superstitious man: he said that slipping into the water was a bad omen and we had better turn back. We would set out again tomorrow, he promised. Having no choice I returned with him. He vanished a short time later. Presumably he changed his mind and decided not to share his hideout with Father and me. If so, he must have gone to the peasant alone or with better potential bunker-mates. The mystery remains unsolved, because I never saw him again or heard anything about him after the liberation. Like many others, he vanished without a trace. Nor did I ever hear again from my cousin Yankl.

Several days later, Berl Goldberg offered to share a hideout with Father and me. Berl had escaped during the march to Siedlce and then spent three weeks hiding in nearby fields and towns. Berl had no money whatsoever.

Our future guardian angel was Jan Zabiniak, a poor villager from Polinów and known for his leftist views. I knew him by sight because whenever he repaired sidewalks in Łosice the children gathered to admire his skillful movements.

Zabiniak lived in Polinów with his young wife and two children in a small house, which they shared with his wife's younger sister. He had a vegetable garden near the Catholic cemetery. Zabiniak let us dig our bunker under the pigsty next to their house. He demanded 1,800 zlotys a month, plus 15 gold rubles for labor and materials for the bunker. We paid for food separately and promised that after the war we would give him whatever we had left, an additional mark of gratitude.

Berl and I visited Zabiniak on the night of November 19, 1942. Zabiniak gave us shovels and we completed the bunker that very night. Although small, it was big enough for three people. We covered the hole with boards, which we camouflaged with two feet of pig manure. Zabiniak made a hatch, two feet to a side, for the entrance to the bunker. We covered it with manure to confuse the gendarmes' dogs.

On Friday, November 20, we left the ghetto and moved into the bunker. We took with us bedding, a kerosene lamp, and whatever clothes we still possessed. We covered the bunker floor with a thick layer of straw that Zabiniak gave us. The place was far from comfortable. We found the stench horrific for the first few days, but soon got used to it. The only good point of our new home was that it was warm.

In Hiding

At first our relations with the Zabiniaks were exemplary. Mrs. Zabiniak brought us food and we all praised her cooking; she was a fine cook. At night, Berl and I often went back to the ghetto to see friends and keep abreast of the news. There was no problem leaving and entering the bunker. Usually we returned within two hours. Sometimes the Zabiniaks visited us in the evenings, bringing food and the latest news from the "free" world. Everything proceeded uneventfully; we prayed that it would continue to do so.

On the morning of November 27, Mrs. Zabiniak rushed to the bunker in a panic. She had been a fool to agree to hide us, she screamed. It was some time before she calmed down sufficiently to explain what had happened. Earlier that morning, German gendarmes and Polish policemen had surrounded the small ghetto and expelled all its inhabitants in the direction of Niemojki. They had killed dozens of people on the road. Now they were fanning out to search for escapees and threatened to kill them along with the families that sheltered them. Mrs. Zabiniak demanded that we leave the bunker at once. We told her that no one knew we were there and the shelter was well hidden. She refused to listen. We understood her situation but had nowhere to go. We were immeasurably worse off now than previously. No Jew could walk the streets safely. We were well known in Łosice and would surely be denounced by anyone who saw us. If we left now, we would be captured on the spot. Soon after that, the Germans would kill us, her, and her entire family. Only after we explained all of this did Mrs. Zabiniak come to her senses.

The week following this incident passed rather quietly. We received food and newspapers. Sometimes our "landlords" visited us at night and spent some time in our company. They reported the latest news — with emphasis on the capture and killing of Jews — but also hinted at every opportunity that we must leave the bunker soon. It was too dangerous, the location was too close to town, too many people circulated in the vicinity, and their young children might babble and inadvertently reveal the secret to a stranger. Even so, we hoped they would allow us to stay on.

One evening, Mrs. Zabiniak brought us a new story. The neighbors already knew about us, she claimed. Again she demanded that we leave the bunker and find a new hideout. We knew she was lying. We reminded her that from the start she had been aware of the peril involved in concealing us and that we were fated to live together until the end of the war. From that day on, Mrs. Zabiniak imposed sanctions on us: the soup she brought us was unsalted or so heavily over-salted as to be undrinkable.

Later she began bringing our meals at irregular hours. Some days we received nothing to eat. On December 16, she again ordered us to leave, this time in such loud tones that we were afraid someone would overhear. We knew we had to go. Father said he would send me out to search for a new hideout the next evening, although we had no idea where to start looking. I asked Mrs. Zabiniak to lend me her sheepskin coat, not only for protection from the cold but also because anyone not dressed in a sheepskin coat looked out of place in a Polish village in the winter, and any stranger was suspected of being Jewish. At first she refused, afraid of losing her coat if I were captured. She finally yielded after I repeated the request several times.

On the frigid night of December 17, I set out in search of a new refuge for the three of us. Father suggested that I visit Mr. Szczebuński on the Woźniki estate. After three weeks of being confined to the bunker, the cold but refreshing air made me light-headed, as though I were drunk. Forcing myself to concentrate on the task at hand, I passed through the dark and empty streets of Łosice before I headed for Woźniki to look up Szczebuński. Since we would encounter each other on many occasions from that time on, I will describe him in detail.

Szczebuński had been working for years as manager of the Woźniki fishponds. He lived on the estate, near the ponds, in a house with an attached garden. He had married a local woman, but my father thought he was of Cossack origin. He was a strong and solid man about forty-five years of age; his wife was somewhat younger. They were childless.

Before the war, every Friday at 3 A.M., Father drove his horse and wagon to the Woźniki estate to buy a barrel of live carp from Szczebuński. He resold the fish to his partners, who in turn sold them to Jewish housewives: every self-respecting Jewish family wanted carp for its Sabbath meal. Father kept up this practice during the first year of the war — it was our main source of livelihood. In the course of his business dealings with Szczebuński, Father had come to respect the man and considered him to be solid and reliable. As I noted above, I had spent some time working under Szczebuński's supervision after the ghetto was instituted. He treated the Jewish laborers very generously. His demands were not excessive and he never beat us. Such behavior was uncommon, because the Germans not only permitted but even encouraged those in his position to abuse their Jewish workers. Szczebuński was a much sought-after employer.

As I walked down the highway toward Woźniki, I suddenly heard footsteps. I was afraid but had no time to hide. I stood up straight and, mustering all my courage, moved into the middle of the road. In the dark I could make out the shapes of two Polish policemen. As they passed one asked whether I had any matches. Without stopping, I answered, "No, I don't smoke."

"Son of a bitch! No one smokes here," one of the policemen grumbled.

The rest of my journey was uneventful.

Szczebuński was frightened when he saw me. A moment ago, he told me, two policemen had visited him looking for concealed Jews. To calm him, I said that I had just seen them leaving for Łosice. His wife crossed herself when she saw me. Two days ago, she said, she had dreamt that my mother asked her to help hide her children. Seizing the opportunity, I said that the dream was a prophecy: I had come to them with precisely this in mind. I told them that Father and I had been hiding out near town but that the neighbors had begun to suspect our benefactors. For that reason, and because those benefactors had children, we had to find a new hideout.

Szczebuński explained that he couldn't hide us. His house was too small, he had no way to conceal us, and his suppliers or customers would eventually catch on. I pleaded: the risk was slight, we were three adults, and our needs were modest. The Germans had been halted at Stalingrad and would soon be defeated. If he were afraid, I added, we could build a bunker some distance away, perhaps near the fishponds. All he had to do was to provide us with food. He said that one of the ponds had been taken out of service before the war because it could not be guarded against nocturnal poachers. The pond had been drained and the fish transferred to other ponds; a little water remained at the bottom but no one approached it. We could build our bunker there.

I accepted his offer happily. We agreed that I would return with a friend on the following day. All I wanted from Szczebuński was a pick and shovels so we could dig the bunker.

Woźniki was run by a hired manager. Before the war, a dirt road crossed it. When the Germans were making their preparation to invade the Soviet Union, they widened the road and surfaced it with gravel and crushed stones so that soldiers could use it to reach the River Bug via Sarnaki. Now, with the front so far away, the Germans hardly used the road. This was a great advantage from our standpoint. The Woźniki estate had several large buildings, a few small houses used by the managers and supervisors, farm buildings, and a vodka distillery. All these structures were near the Szczebuńskis' home. About a third of a mile away, on opposite sides of the road, there were two long buildings where several dozen farmhands and their families lived. The estate also had a large herd of dairy cattle, a lot of arable land, a few patches of forest, and fishponds of various sizes. All the ponds were located between the road and the river, on low terraces, where the River Toczna and its tributaries met the Kaluza.

I returned with Berl the next evening. Overhearing Szczebuński in conversation with someone, we waited outside until 9 o'clock. Finally, I knocked on the door and Szczebuński let us in. There was no mistaking his fear. He told us in so many words that he wanted to renege on his promise. Again we argued with him and downplayed the danger. Eventually he gave in — not because of our powers of persuasion but because of his wife, who repeated the story of her dream. This time she said that, in the dream, my mother had asked her to conceal her children behind the oven and promised her a generous reward in the world to come. To this day, I am convinced that Mother really did protect us.

Szczebuński furnished us with two shovels and an axe and led us to the isolated pond, which was located between the road and a small grove consisting mainly of saplings. For our new shelter we selected a section of the wooden dike around the pond, which had been used to regulate the flow of water. We dug a trench about six feet long, four and a half feet wide, and more than three feet deep. We pruned several saplings to build a roof, which we covered with the rest of the branches. We collected bundles of straw from a pile about 300 yards away and covered the roof with straw and topsoil. We use two planks from the dike for the entrance. It was almost dawn. We hurried back to Father, who was waiting for us in tense anticipation.

The next day, Saturday, December 19, 1942, we told the Zabiniaks that we had found a new hideout and would be leaving that night. We didn't tell them the name of our benefactor or the location of our new refuge. We parted amiably. Zabiniak even hinted that if ever we needed food he would help us. We thanked him for his assistance. We understood their plight — they feared for their fate and that of their children. At about 9 o'clock we packed our belongings and left quickly. We crossed the highway next to the cemetery and ran across the fields to our new hideout. Fortunately, it was very cold and windy and snow began falling. As the saying goes, "You wouldn't even put a dog out in such weather."

When we reached our new bunker we found it in the same condition as we had left it the previous evening. We took several bundles of straw from the nearby pile and laid them on the floor of the bunker. We covered the straw with rags and hung other rags on the walls to keep soil from falling in. We uprooted a sapling from the forest and placed it where the water flowed from the bottom of the dike. We used it as the entrance to the bunker. At sunrise, we pulled the tree in and used it to reinforce the opening, of the two boards we had removed from the dike, which we now returned to their place.

This bunker was much more comfortable than our previous quarters. It was larger and admitted fresh air. The warmth of our bodies quickly heated the interior. We did not expect anyone to search for us during the winter, when in any case the days were shorter. We often took advantage of the darkness to step outside confidently for a breath of fresh air. Although we could not keep abreast of the news as we had with the Zabiniaks, we were happy to have this place and be free.

We paid the Szczebuńskis 600 zlotys a week for food. Six days a week, I visited their house after dark, at around 9 o'clock, and Mrs. Szczebuński gave me a pot of soup she had cooked for us. Sometimes she even added a few chunks of meat to the broth. She invented new recipes regularly and the food was always very delicious. The soup was still hot when I received it but cooled off and congealed by the next morning. Once a week we received two or three loaves of bread to last the week.

We relieved ourselves in a pail, which we emptied at night into the large puddle at the bottom of the pond. We bathed in the spring on the other side of the pond almost every evening. We washed our clothes once a week and hung them to dry overnight on nearby bushes. Since the shelter was heated by the warmth of our bodies, it attracted field mice, which nibbled our bread — a problem we never solved.

Twice Mr. Szczebuński bought gold coins from us, giving us 4,500 zlotys for $20 and 1,800 zlotys for 10 gold rubles. We had no way of finding out whether that was the going rate, but we knew that prices were rising because of the protracted war. We assumed that food prices were climbing more quickly than the price of gold. But we never asked Szczebuński about prices, aware that anyone willing to have dealings with us was taking a risk and would not do so gratis. We expected nothing else, but to this day I believe that Szczebuński was an honest man.

We were certain that other Jews were living in the nearby forests and lacked a hideout. Father said that we could accommodate a fourth person until the spring, and he was sure the war would be over by then. We discussed this with the "Fisherman" (as we called Szczebuński among ourselves), who promised that if he encountered a Jew he would let him join us. About ten days later Berl returned from the "Fisherman" along with our new tenant — Hirsch Wior, whom we had known back in Łosice. He was one of the few to have survived the last stage in the liquidation of Jews in our county. I still remember his story quite well, because he retold it again and again during our lengthy stay in the bunker.

Hirsch Wior was born and grew up in Mlawa, Poland. After World War I, he moved to Berlin, where he worked as a barber. He married and had a son. In November 1938, along with all the Polish-born Jews in Germany, he was deported to Zbąszyń, Poland, and then returned to his hometown, Mlawa. A year later, after the Germans invaded Poland, his family fled toward the Soviet Union but stopped in Łosice for some reason. Wior worked as a barber there until December 1941, when the ghetto was established. Szczebuński was one of his customers. When the large ghetto was liquidated, Wior left Łosice with his family but got separated from his wife and son on the way. He managed to escape from the Mordy area by hiding among the tombstones in the Jewish cemetery. He wandered aimlessly for a few days, eating whatever he found in the fields or asking peasants for handouts. Then, hearing about the small ghetto, he returned to Łosice. For a while I worked with him repairing the road to Woźniki.

Wior believed the notice in the Polish press that Jews would be allowed to live and work in several ghettos in the county, and remained in Łosice until the last day. Shortly before the liquidation, all Jews still working in the vicinity were sent back to the ghetto. Early on the morning of November 27, the ghetto was suddenly surrounded by gendarmes and Polish police. All the residents were taken in a convoy to the Niemojki railroad station. Anyone wearing good clothes was killed en route and his body stripped of clothes and shoes. Jakob Goldfeder, Eliyahu's son, was one of those murdered for their clothes.

In Niemojki, all the Jews were loaded aboard freight cars and transported to Siedlce. From the Siedlce station they were marched to Gęsie Borki, several miles outside of town, where three buildings had been set aside for a new ghetto and another building for Gypsies. Jews from Siedlce and other camps in the area had already arrived there. The Jews of Łosice stuck largely to themselves, though. The first day was bearable. Since the three buildings were left unguarded, people could go out and procure food from the peasants.

Early on the morning of December 3, gendarmes and Polish policemen surrounded the miniature ghetto and ordered everyone to come outside and sit on the ground. After another round of shootings and beatings, the survivors were ordered to form into lines and march to the railroad station. When they reached it they found no cars and were sent back to Gęsie Borki, where they were packed into a single building. It was so cramped that they had to stand up without moving. Some people fainted; others died on their feet. The overcrowding became even worse when workers from various locations were shoved into the same building. Anyone caught looking out a window was shot on the spot. The gendarmes called out several people by name, including some of the Judenrat officials and their families. These people were body-searched and then shot. Next the Polish police singled out people they had done business with in the past. These people met the same fate. For example, the Polish police commander settled scores with Avraham Bressler, the Jewish police chief in the Siedlce ghetto.

A heavy snow fell that night and the searchlights could not pierce the veil. Several Jews seized the moment to climb through windows and escape. The guards fired indiscriminately and continually.

The next morning, all the people were taken out, formed into columns, and sent back to the railroad station. A

German officer named Fabisch announced that they were being sent to work in Minsk Mazowiecki. This calmed people who had been certain they were en route to Treblinka, but it turned out to be just another German lie.

As they waited for the overdue train, the Germans searched anyone who was well dressed and confiscated whatever they turned up. One of the officers ordered Wior to collect money. Fearing summary execution, the deportees gave Wior thousands of zlotys to pay over to the officer. The wait dragged on into the afternoon. The Germans shot many people. The Gypsies hauled the bodies to a nearby pit and stripped them of anything that remained.

The cattle cars came at twilight. After the Germans loaded everyone aboard and locked the doors, the train began to move. Wior was in one of these cars; like all the rest, its windows were boarded over. Realizing now that their final destination was Treblinka, everyone prepared for death. But some passengers made futile attempts to pierce through the boards on the windows with knives or penknives. Then, without warning, a refreshing breeze swept the car.

"The door's open," someone shouted. "Anyone who wants to can jump out!"

Somebody in the car must have had tools and managed to snap the bolt on the door. Wior moved toward the opening but found his way blocked by someone who hesitated to jump. Finally someone shoved the fellow aside and many started leaping out into the darkness.

Wior was one of them. To his good fortune he fell into a

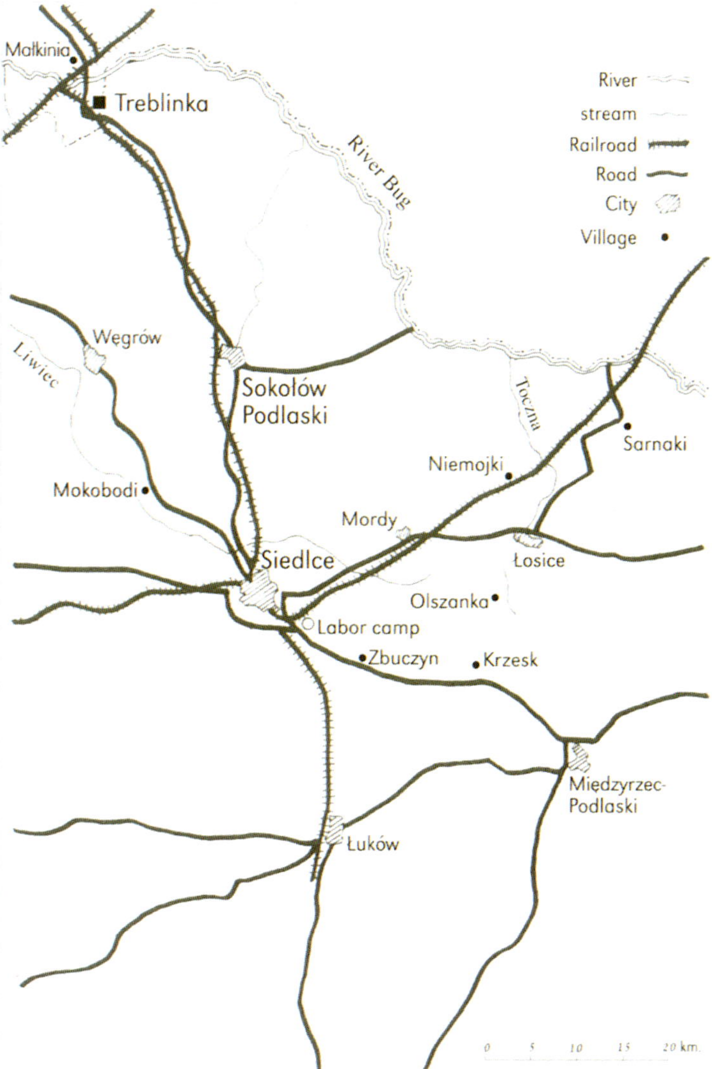

Map of Siedlce area

The author's grandfather, Moshe Zvi Weinstein, and grandmother

The author's mother, Lea, in 1912. She was murdered in Treblinka on August 24, 1942.

The author's Aunt Golda and her husband Peretz. All ten of their children were exterminated.

Deportation of the Jews of Losice, Saturday, August 22, 1942

Notice on the ghetto gate

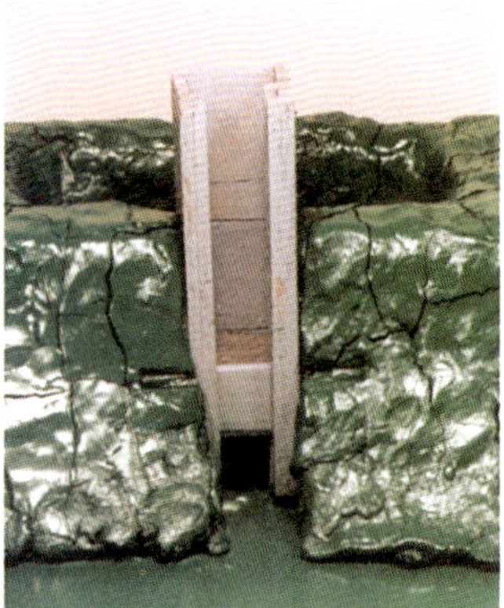

Reconstruction of hideout, sealed

Reconstruction of hideout, open

The author and his friend, Noah Lasman, Losice, October 1944

August 1944, a week after the liberation

Noah Lasman and Edi Weinstein after their discharge from the polish army

The author's father, Asher, and stepmother, Sarah, Windsheim, 1948

Yehuda Weinstein, Windsheim, Germany, 1946

Losice, July 1993. Location of the second ghetto, from August 24, 1942, to November 27, 1942

Edi's marriage to the late Jean Zucker, Windsheim, November 1948

The Jewish cemetery in Losice, April 1991

At the site of the Treblinka camp, July 1993

Edi Weinstein standing on the mound above his hideout, July 1993

snowdrift. The guards on the train shot at him but missed. He raced ahead, hoping to reach the town. Suddenly he heard voices pleading with anonymous assailants not to strip them of their clothing and leave them to freeze to death. Wior realized that the area was full of "hunters" who were pursuing the escapees.

For weeks Wior lived in the fields, staying clear of the villages. Some peasants helped him; others drove him away. Eventually he reached Woźniki and contacted an old acquaintance whom he trusted: Szczebuński. It was Szczebuński. The "Fisherman" greeted him warmly, concealed him for about three weeks, and then sent him to our hideout.

Searching for Food

Our lives in hiding were not free of anxiety. On Saturday afternoon, January 16, 1943, we had a scare when we heard footsteps on the roof of our bunker, accompanied by the barking of dogs. We expected imminent discovery followed by a barrage of bullets. We held our breath and waited for our fate. But we were not exposed and no shots were fired. Whoever it was above our heads had decided to go away. When the sounds faded away and finally stopped we heaved sighs of relief.

That night it was Berl's turn to visit the Szczebuńskis to get our food. Mr. Szczebuński told him that the area was known as a good place in which to hunt hares and that German gendarmes from Siedlce occasionally went there to try their luck. That morning, a worker on a nearby farm had showed them a stable where four Jews were hiding. The Germans captured them and later shot them in Łosice. Szczebuński was terrified by the mere thought that something like that had happened so close to our bunker.

However, we felt safe in our hideout, which was proving itself. The situation on the fronts had turned strongly in the Allies' favor. Massive German forces were dispatched in an attempt to break the siege of Stalingrad. The British defeated the Germans in Libya and the Americans consolidated their control of Morocco and Algeria. Szczebuński did not believe that this marked the beginning of the end. But Wior, claiming to know the German mentality, thought that the German people would rise up against the Nazi regime after so many defeats. We agreed, though eventually we realized that Wior's familiarity with the Germans was deficient.

One night, when I came by to pick up our food, Szczebuński showed me a copy of a Polish underground newsletter with information on Polish units that were fighting in Libya and the German defeats there. I asked whether he could put us in touch with the Polish underground. Although he did not reply, the look on his face told me that Jews were not being allowed to take part in the struggle.

As I returned from the Szczebuńskis' home another evening, I ran into three Jews whom I had known in the small ghetto. If they had no place to hide, I said, they could take shelter in the nearby barn. They laughed at me and said I must be out of my mind. I was glad they did not ask me where I was hiding. People were afraid of one another in those days. No one was a hero. The Germans' methods for breaking people under interrogation and forcing them to talk were well known. When I returned "home," I usually ran about half a mile in the opposite direction, looking over my shoulder all the while, to make sure I was not being followed. Afterwards, I stopped under a tree for a five-minute rest. Only then, convinced that no one was tailing me, did I return to the bunker.

For about ten weeks we kept going to the Szczebuńskis for food. One evening in early March 1943, I crossed the fields toward their house. About 500 yards away I heard people talking and observed someone holding a lantern. Hiding behind the outhouse I saw a horsecart heading toward Łosice. It passed the Szczebuńskis' house, which was about 150 feet from the road. I watched the lantern move in the same direction.

I waited another five minutes before approaching the front door of the house. I was about to open it when Mr. Szczebuński did so from inside. A gendarme rushed out, dragging a woman under his arm. Another gendarme followed and flashed a lantern in my face. Both of them were so drunk they could hardly stand. Although gripped with fear, I did not run. While Szczebuński held the door for them and spoke with them, I stepped inside. Afterwards, Szczebuński escorted them to the road. When he returned, visibly scared, he pushed me out the back door and shouted that I should wait for him near the pigsty.

Somewhat later he came out in a calmer frame of mind and brought me some bread and milk. He was afraid to let me enter the house and explained that, although he had neutralized the gendarmes with large quantities of vodka, I should not come again.

I visited him again a few days later. He was still agitated, believing that someone had denounced him for being involved with Jews. He could think of no other reason for the gendarmes' visit. If that were really so, I tried to explain, the gendarme would at the very least have demanded to see my papers. I thought I had managed to persuade Szczebuński of this, but from that day on he became increasingly fearful. The next time I saw him, three days later, he told me he had to limit his contacts with us. Father's attempts to buy food from acquaintances in a nearby village, Swiniarów, were unsuccessful. Only once did he obtain a slice of bread from the mayor's wife, who, trembling with fear, did not allow him past the front hall and told him flatly not to come back. We decided to turn to Zabiniak, recalling his promise to help us if we needed food.

Our main concern throughout this time was food. We still had $120 and 180 rubles in gold. Although that was considered quite a treasure, we could not find anyone brave enough to sell us food. There was no one to turn to. We trusted no one. Berl volunteered to contact Zabiniak. Zabiniak received him warmly, gave him some bread, and promised to provide additional food the next time he came.

With our Polish money running out, I decided to sell a gold 10-ruble piece. Two weeks later, when Berl visited him again, Zabiniak gave him 1,200 zlotys for this treasure. Although we knew the coin was worth more, we were glad to let Zabiniak get a profit in return for the great risk he was taking on our behalf. Berl returned each time with a few loaves of bread, some butter, kerosene for our lamp, matches, and sometimes newspapers. We appreciated Zabiniak's willingness to resume contact with us and help us. He told us that Miriam Perlmutter had visited him in the middle of January 1943 and asked about us. Disclosing a hideout was considered unwise during the war. I must have mentioned his name to Miriam.

Fortunately, none of us came down with any serious illness. Occasionally one of us had a headache, a cold, or a sore throat, but we dismissed these as trivial. In our circumstances, any more serious illness would have caused indescribable agonies. Once Wior had a severe toothache that caused his gums and cheeks to swell up. When the pain and swelling persisted he wound a piece of string around the tooth and yanked until it came out. The wound bled a little, but the pain and swelling vanished within a day or two. Eventually he recovered and resumed eating in the ordinary way.

As he headed for Zabiniak's house about a week before Easter, Berl encountered a young woman with a girl of about eight. The woman told him that she was part of a group of thirteen Jews who were living in a small forest between Swiniarów and Woźniki. She and her daughter were walking to town, she said, and she would wait on the outskirts while the girl went in to buy bread. Berl and the woman set up a rendezvous in the forest the next night. At that meeting, he conversed with other survivors. They had been hiding on a farm in Swiniarów, but the peasant there began to harass them as soon as their money ran out. Forced to leave, they built a bunker in the nearby forest. All of them were starving and in poor health. Without disclosing the location of his own hideout, Berl set up a third meeting with the woman the next week.

At 7 A.M. on Easter Sunday, we heard gunshots from the direction of the forest. Something terrible had happened, we knew. A week later, we learned the details. Two young Jewish women had gone to Łosice to buy bread. Polish children spotted them and denounced them to some gendarmes who were playing soccer. The gendarmes interrogated the women and held them for several days. On Easter Sunday they took them back to the forest and murdered the entire group.

Berl continued to visit Zabiniak once every two weeks to stock up on supplies and information. Things continued this way for eight weeks, until mid-May. Around then we decided to convert 20 gold dollars into Polish currency. Berl left the coins with Zabiniak and agreed to return a few days later to get our food and money. When Berl returned, however, Zabiniak was not at home and his wife denied all knowledge of his whereabouts. Nor did she offer Berl any food.

We realized that something had gone wrong and were afraid we had made a mistake by giving Zabiniak the coins. When Berl tried again two days later, Zabiniak told him to wait outside.

Zabiniak came back with a shaft from the cart and, without saying a word, began to beat Berl with all his might. Realizing that the Pole meant to kill him, Berl managed to escape somehow.

This incident illustrates the Jews' plight. The Nazis had expelled us from human society. As a result, anyone who did business with us did not feel bound by any law, human or divine. In ordinary times, Zabiniak was an honest man.

But when he found that he could gain easy riches, even at the cost of someone else's life, his honesty evaporated. The Germans managed to evoke this kind of anti-social behavior from people who had been perfectly decent in normal circumstances.

Having lost our source of food, we spent the next ten days subsisting on the grass that grew near the pond. We became weaker and weaker with each passing day and realized that we would starve to death unless we found a solution. Peeping through the cracks in our bunker during the day, we saw workers planting potatoes. One day — it must have been in late May 1943 — Father went out and dug up three-fourths of a pail of tiny potatoes. He filled the pail with water from the well and he and Wior went into the forest. They took rocks from the road, set the pail on them, gathered some dry twigs, and started a fire. Late that night they returned to the bunker with a pailful of half-cooked potatoes. Although we had no salt, we had full stomachs for the first time in several weeks. For us it was a gourmet feast. We repeated the process every night thereafter. Wior and I became practiced cooks. We hung rags around the fire to keep it from being spotted from a distance. As time passed, we got better and better at camouflaging our "kitchen."

When the need arose we would consult with one another about how to improve our situation. Fortunately, I still had plenty of gold coins. Then Berl had an idea. Before the war, his family had lived on the outskirts of town, near the Catholic cemetery. The Miałkowski family lived next door. Mr. Miałkowski was an alcoholic who could sometimes be found stumbling around the market square. We couldn't trust him, but Berl knew his married daughter. The family was terribly poor. One evening in late June, he visited her and offered a considerable sum of money for bread, foodstuffs, salt, and newspapers. She agreed.

At first we gave her 10 gold rubles to convert into Polish currency. When she completed the deal honestly, Berl began to meet her every other week, late at night, to buy food. Later he gave her a $20 gold piece to sell. Two weeks later she gave us our zlotys. The woman always did her best to help us and even gave us pots to cook in. This relationship with Miałkowski's daughter continued for about thirteen months — until the liberation on July 31, 1944.

In 1993, I discovered that her married name was Helena Biernacki. We owe our lives to her and to the Szczebuńskis. It is important to note that the fact that we paid them to help us in no way diminishes their humanity. They placed themselves in terrible danger at a time when no one else was willing to do so.

The Polish and German newspapers they gave us were usually several weeks old, but the news nourished us no less than the bread did. Reports on the progress of the war did wonders for our morale. We interpreted every article and report in the best light possible and concluded that Germany was facing defeat. Like everyone else during the war, we read between the lines and dreamed about Germany's downfall. We analyzed and re-analyzed the reports and sometimes reached erroneous conclusions.

But even the hard news always lifted our spirits. The Germans had been totally expelled from Northern Africa. The Russians had gone over to the offensive on the Kursk front. The Germans were complaining about the "aerial pirates" who raided defenseless German towns. The papers reported the destruction of churches, hospitals, schools, and apartment blocks, but the main targets of the Allied bombing, we realized, were industrial centers. The German townspeople were suffering, but we could feel no sympathy for them. After Italy surrendered, we were sure that Germany would follow suit within a few days.

Before the war, Father was not one of the most devout men in our town, but he prayed every day and wore a full beard. When he fled from the Siedlce camp to the small ghetto, he befriended an old and very pious man whom I knew only as Bezi. Bezi had lost his entire family and was too old to try to hide or escape. He gave Father his old *tallis* and said that if Father wore it while praying each day he would survive the war and witness Germany's downfall. Believing him, Father wrapped himself in the *tallis* every day and prayed quietly. While he did so, the rest of us interrupted our animated conversations and sank into reveries that were not necessarily related to God. However, I also prayed to God quite often, though, asking Him to act on our behalf and keep us alive.

The summer of 1943 passed rather uneventfully. Late each night we went to bathe in the spring and restock our supply of drinking water. Then two of us would go out to gather potatoes and vegetables and the other two would prepare the meal. During the day we stayed in the bunker, peeling potatoes and vegetables, and discussed whatever was on our minds. Berl held his fortnightly meetings with Miałkowski's daughter and returned with provisions and newspapers. We were not hungry; although the meals were terribly monotonous, no one complained. Miałkowski's daughter had given us a small two-burner iron stove and aluminum exhaust pipes.

In September 1943, we dug a second bunker near the place where we did our cooking. It was about four feet wide and five feet deep. We set up the stove there and camouflaged the tiny entrance totally. The tips of the pipes protruded from the bunker to carry off the cooking smoke. We used this bunker to store potatoes, vegetables, and dry branches so we could light a fire on rainy days.

That month, the farmhands began to harvest potatoes from the field next to the bunker. They dug long, shallow trenches to store the potatoes over the winter and covered them up with straw and topsoil. Deciding to appropriate a large stock of potatoes, we dug a third bunker about 150 feet from the second one and closer to the road. One night, the four of us walked back and forth between the trenches and the new bunker and gathered enough potatoes to last the entire winter. Now, in addition to having guaranteed our supper every night, we would be in less danger of discovery because we would not have to emerge every other evening to pilfer or ask villagers for handouts. Father created a primitive grater by puncturing a flat piece of metal with scissors. Now we could grate the potatoes, drain the water through an old rag, add a little salt, and make pancakes on the stove. Those tasted better to us than any yellow cake slathered in whipped cream could have.

Sometime in late October 1943, the cows on the estate ran out of pasturage and were brought to graze near our bunker. When one of the beasts stopped directly overhead, she bent our ceiling out of shape. The four of us had to prop it up until the cow was so kind as to move on. That night, we ventured out and reinforced the bunker with stronger planks than we had used before, and then covered it with fresh soil.

There was some danger in this, because now the area above the bunker was bare dirt. But we knew that peril lurked everywhere. We often remarked to each other that we might die at any moment. Although we felt relatively safe, since only Szczebuński knew where the main bunker was, we were afraid that the farmhands' children would discover our kitchen bunkers while they were foraging in the forest for mushrooms. So, despite our confidence, we were very cautious. We were especially careful to erase our traces, leaving the ground as it had been before our excavation work and camouflaging the entrance to our bunkers with leaves and branches.

Newspapers in Polish and German were an inexhaustible source of topics for conversation. The worldliest person in our group was Wior, who had spent almost half his life in Berlin. Father was worldly, too, but in a different way. His service in the Tsar's army had broadened his knowledge of countries and peoples that were part of the Russian Empire — exotic and enchanting topics for me. Wior predicted a putsch in Germany. Berl was usually pessimistic and kept saying that we had no chance of surviving the war. Eventually someone would spot us and denounce us to the authorities, he said. We should also beware of Polish children, Berl said, reminding us of the fate of the two young women. Time and again he said that he envied birds and dogs, which retained their right to live because they were of concern to no one. Unlike Berl, I believed that we would come through. I argued that if I had managed to escape from the very core of the inferno — Treblinka — after having been wounded there, I was evidently destined to live. Father always seconded me in this belief.

When I recall those conversations today, I have to admit that Berl had logic on his side. Our prospects of survival really were quite poor. Today I know that most of those who escaped from the small ghetto did not survive. The fallacy, though, was applying normal terms to estimating one's chances of survival in such chaotic times. The Germans had created absurd circumstances. The hatred and cruelty they manifested toward all the occupied peoples were difficult to understand, even in terms of their own interests. Their conduct only swelled the ranks of their enemies. It was also illogical to exterminate the Jews, since these millions of human beings, some of whom possessed crucially needed skills, could have benefited Germany's war effort.

We found it difficult to think about plans for the post-liberation future, perhaps because deep down we doubted that we would live to see that day. Wior thought he would return to Mlawa and hoped that his acquaintances would be pleased to see him again. It had not yet dawned on us that the people who had seized our homes and furniture would not give us a warm welcome. We knew we could not remain in a town where all of our acquaintances had been murdered. Post-liberation Łosice would never be our home, we realized, even though our forebears had lived there for hundreds of years.* My father's older brother had gone to the United States decades earlier and obtained American citizenship. We were sure he would send us visas for the United States. However, these thoughts were no more than daydreams against the backdrop of our bunker, the empty fishpond, and the young forest, which were our entire world.

The winter of 1943/44 came late and, when it did come, was largely free of frost and snow. This was good for us, because footprints in the snow might be dangerous. In late March 1944, as spring was about to begin, we read in a German newspaper that the Wehrmacht had invaded Hungary and that a pro-Nazi regime had been installed in Budapest. The new government there was even more subservient to the Third Reich than its predecessor had been; it enforced the Nuremberg Laws and sealed the Budapest ghetto. I was astonished by this turn of events. For eighteen months we had been certain that the fate of Jews under fascist governments throughout Europe resembled their fate in Poland and Germany. Although the German press dealt intensively with Jews and accused us of every crime imaginable, including responsibility for the eruption of World War II, it never hinted that Jews

* See Appendix B.

were still living in Europe, let alone in normal circumstances. Of course, neither did we imagine that before its defeat the Nazis would be able to murder so many Hungarian Jews, as well as others who had fled to Hungary from elsewhere.

One night in early March 1944, when Wior and I went to cook, we found our mess bunker in ruins — potatoes and vegetables strewn everywhere, the kitchen demolished. We suspected that somebody might be lying in ambush for us. Cautiously we backed away and spent the next half-hour observing the area. During our fifteen months underground we had hardly ever emerged in broad daylight and had developed senses similar to those of forest creatures. Had anyone been nearby, we would have noticed him because we knew the surroundings well and our eyes had become as accustomed to the dark as if we were nocturnal animals. We would also hear any pine needle that happened to fall.

When we returned to the mess bunker, we were astonished to find our kitchen utensils strewn on the ground as far as the edge of the forest, near the road. Again we concealed ourselves among the trees and waited for a long time, but no one came. We figured that the Germans had discovered our bunker; had villagers been the culprits, they would surely have removed the potatoes, vegetables, and stove, since such items were very valuable to them. We gathered up the pieces of our stove and moved them to the bunker where we stored potatoes for the winter. Since it was almost spring and our supplies were dwindling, that bunker had room for the stove, too. For safety's sake, however, we did not start a fire for the next few days.

Eventually we went back to cooking every other evening and, some time later, every evening apart from Friday night — the Sabbath.

When spring came, military activity on the front intensified. According to German reports, the Russians had already crossed the pre-war Polish frontier near the Polesie marshes. At night, far-off explosions — Russian shelling, we assumed — shook the ground. All the evidence suggested that the front was moving toward us. Our hopes of surviving until liberation rose.

Work in the fields was not affected by the nearness of the front, but it was suspended in April 1944 by a bout of severe frost. When work finally began, we peered through the cracks and saw two farmhands plowing the potato field with two pairs of horses. The next day, the workers returned and began to labor near "our" pond. At around 10:00 A.M., we heard footsteps near our bunker and a light tapping at the entrance. One of the workers, speaking in Polish, noted that there wasn't any grass here — it must be an opening to a bunker. As he said this he stepped up his pounding on the two boards we had removed from the dike.

"Boys, stop it!" I shouted at them in Polish. Frightened, the workers fled with their horses and plows. We ran after them, shouting at them to come back. Just then they seemed to recognize Father. We told them to return to work; we would pay them, we said, for keeping mum and not disclosing our presence. We were agitated and frightened. Before this incident, only Szczebuński, whom we trusted, knew we were there. Now we were afraid that the farmhands would return with police or gendarmes.

The laborers returned at dusk. I gave each of them 100 zlotys and asked them not to tell anyone about us. After the war, I promised, we would sell my grandfather's property and give them the proceeds. I asked how they had discovered our location. They said they had noticed trampled grass near the pond and potato and vegetable peels by the spring. They took these to be clear indications that someone was around — certainly a trespasser. During the two days they spent plowing the field, they also noticed that no grass grew on top of the dike. Since the boards were old, though, they inferred that no one had been there lately. At first, mistaking us for partisans, they were afraid. We asked them to return the following Tuesday with some bread and milk.

A week of severe anxiety followed. We knew that sooner or later we would have to abandon our bunker, because somebody was sure to denounce us to the Germans. But we had nowhere else to go. We wanted to believe that as long as we paid them off, the farmhands would treat us as well as they treated their cows. And since the Russians were advancing, we believed our new friends would not inform on us.

The farmhands came back at the appointed time, bringing the food we had asked for. Again I gave each of them 100 zlotys. They visited us three more times with small amounts of bread and milk and always received money in return. They told us terrible stories about the fate of other Jews. Each time they met us they reported about two, three, four, or five Jews who had been captured in the nearby forests, farms, and fields, and brutally murdered. Their purpose in telling us this, we knew, was to terrify us. At the same time they praised our bunker, its construction, and its convincing camouflage. Perhaps they did not wish to lose their new source of income by causing us to seek refuge elsewhere.

One night in early May 1944, we found our storage bunker demolished. The branches on top had been scattered and the stove and our victuals had vanished. Obviously some local people, perhaps our new "friends," had got inside. Since it was already spring, we decided to do our cooking as we had the previous year — in the forest.

Two days later, at about three o'clock on a Sunday morning, we were busy organizing for the coming day when we heard footsteps on the roof of the bunker and, afterwards, a tapping on the entrance. It was Szczebuński; he had come to warn us that the farmhands were talking about the hidden Jews. He advised us to leave and look for a hideout somewhere else. The Russians were close and would arrive soon, he said. Until they did, we could surely survive somehow. We thanked him and he went away.

He was right, of course, but we had nowhere to go. Our hideout was comfortable and well stocked. If we left the area, we would encounter new and serious problems. So we decided to dig a new bunker in the forest. Berl and I chose a site not far from the demolished bunker but closer to the main road, in a dense copse of new growth. We went to work immediately, being even more cautious than with the previous bunkers. We camouflaged the location as best we could. To mask our traces, we carried the soil we had excavated to a distance and covered it with leaves so it would not look recently disturbed. We were especially careful to conceal the entrance.

After three days of labor, the bunker was ready. Wior, distrustful of the two farmhands, moved there at once. The rest of us tried to think rationally and concluded that we had no reason to fear them as long as they were getting money from us. They visited us again about a week later, on a Tuesday. Wior was at the new bunker; he preferred to live there and to visit us for about an hour after nightfall. Berl had gone off to obtain bread. Thus, Father and I were alone. To set the stage for the scene to follow, one of the farmhands pretended to be drunk. The two told us new atrocity stories about Jews who had been caught and murdered nearby. Then, as always, I handed 100 zlotys to each of them. But when I gave the money to the one who was "intoxicated," he called out, "Why only 100 zlotys? I want 100,000! If I don't get it, I'll go to the gendarmerie, you Jew sons of bitches!"

Although frightened, I pretended to laugh. "You must be joking," I said. "Where would we get that kind of money? After the war, we'll sell my grandfather's house and property and the two of you will get *more* than 100,000 zlotys." He insisted that he would go to the gendarmerie anyway. "If you come here with gendarmes," I retorted, "I'll tell them that you've known about us for a long time and you've been providing us with food. They'll finish you off along with us."

He lunged forward and tried to strike me. Father, in tears, begged them to wait until he could contact his acquaintances in the village and ask them to sell his father's house and bring them the money. The "sober" farm worker restrained the "drunk" one. They agreed to return on Saturday night to pick up the sum they had demanded. As soon as they went away, Wior arrived, immediately followed by Berl, who brought provisions and newspapers. The four of us moved to the new bunker that night. Before we left, we caved in the ceiling — the section that had been propped up since the cow trod on it — and covered the bunker over with dirt.

This happened in the middle of May 1944. Immediately noticing how congested and cramped the new bunker was, we improved its ventilation by creating two vent holes near the trees. At night we stepped outside for fresh air, but like moles returned to our burrow before dawn. The last man in had to camouflage the entrance totally and cover it with twigs and leaves. To reduce the danger of discovery, we cooked every other day. The greedy farmhands never found us. They must have thought we had fled far away.

Once every two weeks, Berl brought food and newspapers from the Miałkowskis, as before. In this fashion we learned that the Russians had occupied Volhynia and Polesie — provinces that had belonged to Poland before the war. Now the fighting raged in the vicinity of Kowel, not far from the River Bug. More and more often we heard the echoes of bomb explosions and the noise of aircraft overhead. The newspapers, too, were filled with stories about the "heroic" feats of the defenders of the New Order at Normandy, where the Allied armies had landed. The Allies' resolve to liberate both Eastern and Western Europe raised our morale. If we could survive for another month or two, we knew, we would witness Germany's downfall and be free again.

Liberation

On Saturday night, July 29, 1944, we crawled out of the bunker to the deafening cacophony of heavy vehicles accompanied by vigorous shouts in German. We realized at once that the Germans had decided to mount a stand against the advancing Russians near our forest, which was on higher ground than the rest of the area. We were no more than seven or eight miles from the River Bug, where, we assumed, the retreating Germans might establish a new defensive line. Father was concerned that our hideout was too close to the Germans for us to stay there. Sooner or later soldiers would discover us, he warned; we had to get away before the retreating Germans could dig in nearby. Berl and I agreed with him. Wior, however, decided to stay, arguing that it was more dangerous to wander in the fields and that the German troops probably would not stay long. We decided that each of us would follow his own instincts. We divided the bread up and filled several bottles with water. Then Father, Berl, and I left the bunker.

We crossed the forest in the darkness, slipping between the trucks, and made our way to the fields on the slope. We crossed the road and stopped about six hundred yards beyond it, and roughly twice as far from the forest. Drying sheaves of grain stood in the fields. We did not want to go too far from the bunker, since we might want to go back if we felt safe. We had long since stopped trusting the locals and were as afraid of them as of the Germans. A peasant might identify us as Jews, try to blackmail us, or turn us over to the Germans, who — notwithstanding their current preoccupation with the Russians — would surely enjoy the opportunity to murder three more Jews.

We spent that night hiding among the sheaves. At 9 the next morning — Sunday, July 30, 1944 — we crawled out to eat and immediately went back to hiding in the grain. Soon after, we heard the roar of motorcycles and shouts in German from the direction of the road, which, as I said, was about six hundred yards from us. Soldiers leaped off the motorcycles and began running toward us. We fled for our lives, each in a different direction. Near the grain field was a potato field. I found myself a furrow and wriggled on my stomach toward the road, hoping that the Germans would not search so close to the motorcycles. I lay motionless for a long time, unable to see a thing. It was late at night before I dared stand up.

At about 11 P.M., I threaded my way back to the field where the three of us had been hiding. I noticed that all the sheaves had been scattered. In the direction of Swiniarów, however, there were fields of rye that had not yet been harvested. In despair, convinced that Father and Berl had been captured and shot, I walked along the trampled path, hoping only to find their bodies. After advancing several hundred yards, I came upon a reaper that the villagers of

Swiniarów had left behind. When I came up to it, I suddenly heard someone whisper my name: "Yidl, Yidl!" It was Father. We fell into each other's arms and cried soundlessly for some time. We had each been sure that the other was dead. Father had taken shelter among the sheaves, he told me. The Germans had scattered almost all of them, but miraculously skipped his. He had not moved since then. I think that Berl must have been shot as he tried to escape; by behaving as he did he saved our lives. Now Father and I moved away, detouring around the main road and the forest, which were full of Wehrmacht soldiers, and moving toward the fishponds and the town of Chuchleby, on the eastern bank of the creek.

At dawn, we reached a field that was part of the Woźniki estate and had not yet been reaped. Exhausted by the hardship of the previous day we lay down to rest in a spot where the rye grew tall and thick. We still had a small bottle of water and a loaf of dry bread. Soon the shooting around us became so intense that we feared for our lives. Imagine, we told each other, after everything we had gone through, being hit by a stray bullet now, on the eve of liberation.

At about 9 A.M. we heard a loud noise, followed by the pounding of soldiers' boots. They were looking for us, we figured. A spotter, perhaps in a treetop, must have noticed us and mistaken us for enemy soldiers or partisans. Panic-stricken, we sat there motionless and listened to the approaching footsteps. Within seconds one of the soldiers noticed us and summoned his comrades. We stood up and were immediately surrounded by at least fifteen soldiers, all aiming their rifles directly at us. The *Feldwebel* (sergeant) ordered them to take us to the nearby field. Knowing the Germans, we were sure we were going to be killed.

"What are you doing in the field?" the sergeant asked.

I answered him in German, "We had jobs with the gendarmerie in Łosice, but since the outpost was evacuated we've been looking for farm work during harvest season. When the barrage of gunfire began suddenly we dropped down in the grain to keep from being hit." I felt as though someone had put the words into my mouth.

"Yes, but why in the grain?" he pressed.

It was so thick, I explained, that it might slow the bullets before they reached our spot in the middle of the field. When they heard this, they burst into laughter — a wholehearted, uninhibited, childlike laughter that went on and on. A few of them patted each other on the hip; others slapped comrades' shoulders. One of them shouted, "*Wunderbar! Solche dumme Kerl! SO naiv!**" But I really believed it.

The sergeant and a few soldiers conferred about what to do. Our fate was on the line, we knew. When the discussion was over, he ordered a young soldier to escort us to the road. The others walked off in the opposite direction. At first, we thought he had been ordered to shoot us. I whispered to Father that we should try to jump him when I gave a sign. When we approached the road, however, we

* "Fantastic! What an idiot! So naive!"

saw two large tanks. Obviously we could not carry out my plan. The soldier led us to the road, which was empty of traffic, and ordered us not to hide in the fields again. The best thing we could do, he said, was go back to town. Then, without another word, he left us alone, perhaps wishing to return to his comrades. We were alone and alive. We could not believe it!

In the meantime, the shooting from the east became more intense. The soldier had left us at a point directly across from the pond, near our first bunker and not far from the bunker where Wior might still be hiding. We were afraid to walk toward Łosice because we knew we would have to cross the forest where the Germans had set up an artillery battery. Instead, we decided to crawl on our bellies across the potato field to the spring that had been our only source of water for two years. Hiding among the shrubs, we noticed a soldier observing the area from a treetop about fifty yards away. This was evidently how we had been spotted in the rye field. Another soldier was standing at the foot of the tree. We went up to them and explained that their comrades had found us on the other side of the main road and told us to walk to Woźniki.

The soldiers found this explanation reasonable. Under their watchful gaze we picked some peas in the field nearby their lookout and then continued to walk toward the estate. We tried not to get too close to the farm itself because the workers there, and especially our two would-be blackmailers, might identify us. We crossed a dirt road that led to Woźniki and entered the estate through the pond area.

Just then, the firing resumed, but heavier than before. We crossed the main road again, this time near a burning tank, and climbed onto a high embankment. After running about 300 yards, we realized that we had no chance of surviving here. We climbed down from the embankment and ran toward the creek that separated us from Chuchleby. We lay there for about an hour until the shooting stopped. Looking up, we saw five soldiers at the top of the hill, clutching machine guns primed for use. Their uniforms were different from those of the Germans — Russian, I presumed. The soldiers came down the slope, apparently intending to ford the stream. I stood up and shouted at them in Polish: they could get across by stepping on stones. I made my point with the help of sign language. An officer followed by four soldiers crossed the shallow creek and listened to what I was saying.

"Where have the Germans gone?" the officer asked.

Father could not restrain himself any longer. He raced toward them, shouting, "*Wy, Russkiye?*" — "You are Russians?" — and kissed and hugged them. The Red Army had already occupied the estate and the town, they said. Without hesitation, they led us to the farm, where a Russian officer gave us a cordial welcome, ordered his soldiers to feed us, and asked who we were.

"We are Jews who have been hiding from the Germans," Father replied in Russian.

This first encounter with the Russians, which assured us our freedom, took place near the village of Chuchleby, next to Kaluza Creek. It was about 2 o'clock on Monday afternoon, July 31, 1944. I will always consider this date as meaningful as the day of my birth. Father felt the same way: when people asked him how old he was, he used to say he was born on July 31, 1944.

Father stayed behind at the estate; I set out to look for Wior to see if he was still alive. Because the shooting had not yet stopped, I ran the whole way in the ditch next to the road. Leaving the ditch by the forest I saw — though from a distance — that the area near the bunker had not been damaged. This made Wior's survival more likely; the thought boosted my spirits. When I finally reached the bunker, I found Wior, safe and sound. He had not ventured from the bunker since we had left. I told him that he was a free man and could leave the bunker for good. We returned to the estate and spent the night there.

The next morning, the three of us walked the three miles to Łosice. Villagers from Swiniarów, working in the fields along the way, told us that there were still many Jews in Łosice. We thought this somewhat unlikely. In fact, we found fifteen Jews in our hometown; others who trickled in during the next few days brought the total to twenty-five.

This was the price of the years of murder. In 1942, there had been about 8,000 Jews in the ghetto, most of them from Łosice and others from Sarnaki and nearby villages, in addition to refugees and deportees from western Poland and Warsaw.

Some of the twenty-five survivors were originally from Łosice; others came from Sarnaki, Poznan, Blaszki, Kalisz, and Warsaw. In 1942, the ghettos and camps in Siedlce County had a combined Jewish population of

35,000-40,000; by the time the Red Army arrived, only about 200 of us survived.

All the survivors lived together in a two-story building on the market square, which had once been the property of Joseph Zajfainder. After the Jews had been murdered, the building was occupied by people who bore the opprobrium of collaborating with the Germans. They chose to move out before the Red Army came in. The building was empty and unfurnished, but this did not bother us. For the first two weeks, we all slept on the floor. We ate together and made do with whatever we could find, mainly dry bread and potatoes.

We thought we were out of danger and that antisemitism had vanished along with the occupier. On our first night at home, however, unknown assailants threw a grenade into the corridor and shouted, "Death to the Jews." Fortunately, none of us was injured because the front hall was empty. Still, the incident made us fearful and anxious.

Gedalia Rosenzweig and Michael Fischmann, with whom I had escaped from Treblinka, did not return from their hiding places. The other people living in the building with us had survived in conditions similar to ours. Most had hidden in the fields or forests; several, in a barn or pigsty. Their experiences were similar to ours, too. Some told about comrades in a hideout who had died; others, about companions who had gone out to look for food but did not return, and must have perished in unknown circumstances. All spoke of acts of murder, blackmail, flight, hunger, the need to keep moving to a new place, and sick people who were afraid to contact a doctor. It was true: anyone who fell ill and wasn't strong enough to recover on his or her own had no chance of surviving. In one forest bunker, a woman gave birth and her husband had to strangle the baby with his own hands, because it could not possibly survive in their hideout and would have endangered the others. The mother was still in mourning and beset with guilt feelings, but all of us understood and showered her with love.

Two of the survivors were a woman and her fifteen-year-old niece, both from Kalisz, who had leaped from a train en route to Treblinka. As they ran, a guard shot the woman in the eye. The two of them found refuge with a villager, who sheltered them until the liberation. Then the peasant announced his intention of marrying the girl, but she fled with her aunt and reached Łosice.

There were also two sisters and a girl of about eight from Tluszcz, a town near Warsaw, who managed to elude the Nazi murder machine by posing as Polish servants on an estate in Patków. Another woman survived by working on a farm and posing as a deaf-mute to mask her Yiddish accent. To compensate for her years of silence, she now chattered incessantly. Another survivor had been concealed by a member of a religious sect who treated all Jews as though they were his older brothers.

Goldstein the grocer, my former employer, had been hidden, along with other people, by a peasant near Konstantinów, who received a hefty subvention for this service. Several weeks after the liberation, the man was murdered for having concealed Jews. In the same vicinity, the Łosice family (husband, wife, and three children) survived, as did the Pinkus family (husband, wife, and two children; their first-born daughter was murdered). They had hidden in a bunker under a pigsty.

Aryeh Lieberman, along with his brother and two cousins, had also hidden under a pigsty on a farm in return for a monthly payment to the farmer. One night, as they were about to step out for fresh air, the peasant and his family began to pour boiling water on them. Aryeh escaped with minor burns. One of his cousins also managed to get out of the bunker but was blinded by the boiling water. Crazed with pain, he ran through the village streets, shouting for someone to lead him to the German police. After he gave the Germans the facts, they led him back to the farm, killed the peasant and Aryeh's cousin, and set the house ablaze. Aryeh's brother and his other cousin never returned; evidently they had been scalded to death.

Some peasants reacted to the discovery of a Jew by trussing him up and delivering him to the gendarmerie. For this they received five kilograms of sugar, the standard bounty for the head of a Jew. Almost all those who concealed Jews demanded stiff payment for the risks they incurred. After the liberation, however, most of these benefactors asked the Jews to cut their ties with them and not let on that they had helped them. They were afraid of the Armia Krajowa, the Polish "People's Army."

Several days after the liberation, Mr. Pinkus was visited by Roman Perski, a Polish refugee from Poznan. Perski had in tow a Jewish girl about five years old, a member of the Wajman family, who wanted to join other Jewish survivors. She was accepted at once, of course, and the woman from Kalisz volunteered to look after her. The girl related that her mother had been denounced by a blacksmith named Korsak and murdered by gendarmes as she looked on. Her cousins, also hiding in town, had also fallen victim to informers and been shot by the Germans. Later they were buried in the Jewish cemetery.

Also with us was a boy named Smolarz, who had survived alone by hiding in the woods near the village of Majówka. His family, who had hidden near Laskowice, were murdered by the people who concealed them. Israel Goldstein, who witnessed the murder, conveyed the facts to the boy. Unfortunately, Goldstein did not survive either. A peasant murdered him several hours before the liberation.

Jakob Müller showed up a few days later. The last time I had seen him, in Treblinka, he was being led toward the crematoria along with another 199 or so Jews. When he got there, however, he was put to work cremating the bodies of the other victims. In August 1943, the worker-prisoners at Treblinka staged an uprising. They killed several SS men, broke through the fences, and escaped. The guards in the watchtowers shot down most of them. Later, at the end of the war, newspaper accounts indicated that about thirty of the rebels had survived. The death factory was not returned to service after the uprising; all those transported there afterwards were employed in removing the evidence. They looked for bodies and other traces of the mass graves, burned them, and scattered the ashes in the surrounding fields.

After the vicinity of Węgrów and Sokolów was liberated, many Jews emerged from their hideouts and returned to their towns — only to be threatened with brutal death if they did not immediately move on. Throughout the liberated areas, Jewish survivors were afraid to go outside the city limits. For several months after the liberation no Jew in Łosice had the temerity to demand the restitution of his apartment, house, or factory. Property claims were not filed until later.

Nevertheless, a sense of stability settled in. In Łosice, the Russians established a command center and ordered the residents to go there and hand over any weapons in their possession. Not everyone obeyed the order, but we felt safer after townspeople bearing rifles and wearing armbands vanished from the streets.

Several days later, an induction notice appeared. The members of the small group of Jewish survivors vacillated about whether to join the Polish army after all the hardships they had endured. As always, each of us made his own decision. Of the six men who received notices, only two were actually inducted — myself and Noah Lasman, a refugee from Poznan who had been separated from his family and survived under conditions similar to ours.

In Polish society, too, the question of induction had become the talk of the town, but for different reasons. Young Poles had contacts with organizations that answered to the Polish government-in-exile in London. Accordingly, they expected the pre-war regime to be reinstated and believed they would resume the lifestyle they had known in the past. Their underground organizations ordered them to refrain from helping to rebuild their country and to resist induction into the "Communist" Polish army. Jews who had managed to survive the inferno, in contrast, simply wished to defeat the Germans, whatever the source of the weapons for accomplishing this. Nor did I have any particular objection to a redistribution of land or a westward realignment of Poland's borders after the defeat of Germany.

Before I joined the army, a villager from Swiniarów who was working in the fields found Berl's body. We took it to the Jewish cemetery and buried it in accordance with Jewish tradition. Unfortunately, the list of victims continued to grow after the liberation. Although the Germans were gone, many locals were delighted to keep solving the Jewish problem by murder. If the Germans could kill us with impunity, they figured, so could they.

Epilogue

After a hasty basic training, my company was sent to Lubartów, where we inspected the papers of every passing vehicle. At that time, the Vistula River was still the front. After the January 1945 offensive, however, we advanced through Warsaw, Lodz, western Poland, Western Pomerania, and Lower Silesia and fought in Upper Saxony until the end of the war. We were pleased that the war was now being waged on German soil and that Germany was being punished for the suffering it had inflicted on others. We saw tens of thousands of German PoWs and observed in the eyes of these people, formerly so haughty, the same stark fear that had been in the eyes of the inhabitants of Poland during five long years of occupation. Now every soldier condemned his government's actions. Even SS men, revealed as such by their tattoos, shed crocodile tears and claimed that they had been drafted into the corps in which they had served and had done so against their will. Deep down, they had always rejected the Nazi ideology, they maintained.

The survivors who stayed behind in Łosice and all the small towns nearby fell victim to an additional wave of murder, this time carried out by Poles. After the January offense, large Soviet-Polish formations moved far to the west. Consequently, the area between the Bug and Vistula rivers became lawless. The Polish underground seized the opportunity to resume its operations — this time mainly against Jewish survivors. On the night of March 11, 1945, Polish "patriots," members of the Armia Krajowa (AK), stormed Łosice, Mordy, and Mokobody, searching for Jews. The Jews in Łosice knew they were in mortal peril and hid. But the A.K. men murdered eleven of twenty survivors in Mordy and seven of fifteen in Mokobody. Even women and children were not spared. A young man from Łosice, killed in Mordy, had been the only survivor of a large extended family. His name was Herschel Wolker.

In these small towns, the Jews had taken no interest in politics and were not associated with any political organization, let alone the authorities. They were simple people, artisans and petty merchants, who only wanted to make a living. All their efforts were directed toward holding out until the war was over and then making contact with relatives abroad who could help them leave Poland and start over elsewhere. After that night, all the surviving Jews in small towns in the county moved to Siedlce, mostly in army trucks, and continued via ruined Warsaw to Lodz, which had also been liberated by then.

In August 1945, while I was stationed near Wloclawek to guard a group of locked railroad cars, my battalion ordered me to report to Warsaw for a permanent appointment as company quartermaster. Since I had to pass through Lodz on the way, I decided to visit Father and other survivors I knew, all of whom were living in one building at 17 Narutowicza Street. This is when I discovered why they had left Łosice, learned about the Jews who had been murdered in Mokobody and Mordy, and heard that Poles were throwing Jews from moving trains.

With that, I made up my mind to leave the Polish army. I served my homeland loyally until the end of the war, but, having lost my mother, my brother, four uncles, and five aunts (one of whom perished along with her ten children), I concluded that it was time to get out of Poland. I wanted to start life over, get married, and establish a family that would carry on the Weinstein name. Father and I took a train to Walbrzych, in Lower Silesia, and from there, with packs on our backs, we crossed Czechoslovakia and Austria and reached occupied Germany. We lived in a DP camp at Bad Windsheim until July 1949, when we finally completed the paperwork and left for the United States.

We stayed in touch with Szczebuński, who had relocated to Szczecin. We sent him parcels and money frequently until we heard that he had passed away. Father died of old age in 1972. To his last day, he kept the *tallis* he had been given in the small ghetto. In our bunker he had wrapped himself in it every day to recite his prayers, and it was his most treasured possession. At his request, I buried him in that *tallis*.

I married in the DP camp in Germany in 1948. My wife and I raised two children, both of whom graduated from university and established families. My greatest pleasure today is to play with my seven grandchildren. My older son, Larry, received his Ph.D. in biochemistry at the University of Colorado; my younger son, Michael, is a professor of mathematics at the University of Michigan. I thank God every day for allowing me to live, since 1949, in a country where people's fate is determined by themselves and not by their religion or origin.

I often recall the days and events that I have described here. For many years I wanted to go back and see the country where I was born and the places where I had hidden. But the political situation in Poland made tourism unfeasible. After the sweeping political changes in Eastern Europe in the late 1980s, the gates of many countries that had barred tourists were opened to the West. Thus I was able to return to Poland in July 1993, in the company of my wife and my son Michael.

In Warsaw we hired a taxi and set out for Łosice via Siedlce. In brilliant sunshine we retraced the route on which, fifty-one years earlier, we had been driven like cattle to Siedlce, en route to our death in Treblinka. The handful of Jews who survived that experience called that bitter day "Black Sabbath." As we approached Stock Laski, my eyes began to water. I recalled the moment when I last saw my mother, walking behind the horsecarts and being led away.

The route had not changed. The road was still narrow, but now it was fully paved and in good condition, with no potholes. The wooden houses that once lined the road, with their thatched roofs, had vanished. All the homes visible now were made of bricks. We stopped in Mordy, halfway to Łosice. The market square in that small town had been totally transformed. The pavement was of asphalt instead of flagstones. The square, always bustling when I was young, was empty. Farther on, we passed the Pilsudski mound. In 1935, my school had taken part in a memorial ceremony for the marshal, the hero of Polish independence. The forest near the town of Majòwka was older than it had been when the children of Łosice spent happy summers there so many years ago.

Łosice had grown. Near the road to Siedlce, several buildings occupied an area that had once been farmland. I realized there was no chance of meeting old acquaintances. Before the war, 80 percent of the 6,000 inhabitants had been Jewish. Most of them had perished in the war; the rest were gone — dead or moved away. Most of the 7,000 people in Łosice today were born after I left, to parents who settled there after the war. Apart from a few elderly townspeople, no one remembered the Jews of Łosice at all.

We crossed the bridge and entered the town by Siedlecka Street. I recognized some of the buildings. On the left, however, I noticed a relatively new spacious and handsome two-story structure that (as the sign informed us) housed the town authorities. We passed the church, which looked smaller than I remembered it. In general, all the buildings seemed smaller than my imagination and the distance of time had portrayed them.

We stopped where the market square used to be, next to a shop that was once Mr. Kowalski's pharmacy. I was surprised to discover that the paved square was gone, replaced by attractive greenery; trees and bushes lined the asphalt paths. On the other side, there was a small monument to the May 3 constitution. I recalled having read in Oskar Pinkus's book *House of Ashes* that a memorial plaque to the murdered Jews was to have been installed there, but I could not find it. People whom I asked did not know. Finally, somebody remembered that the square had been renovated many years ago. The plaque must have been removed back then. Where is it now?, I asked. Nobody could tell me.

There were only a few shops in the square, in marked contrast to the many peddlers and buyers I recalled from my childhood. The street signs, too, seemed strange. When I was young, no one needed them. Surprisingly, our car did not attract attention. Before the war, trucks came through daily; but a private car stopping at the market square would have caused excitement and lured a crowd of curious children and adults. The indifference we experienced now may have been the clearest indication of the progress that Łosice has made. After circling the square, we walked down Bielska Street toward the place where I was born. The house was gone. Many of the old buildings on the street, mainly those made of wood, had been torn down. Nearby on the left stood a large, new, concrete apartment block. As we walked down the street, I told my wife and Michael about the houses that had once stood there, the people who inhabited them, what they did for a living, and what they were like.

On Miedzyrzecka Street, the site of the great synagogue was occupied by new buildings. I asked two old men if they remembered my father. Suspiciously they asked whether

I had returned to demand the restitution of our house. I answered in the negative and added that my parents had been renters. They were relieved to hear this and took a slightly more favorable attitude toward us.

I no longer wished to wander along the side streets. I was afraid. Instead, we drove to Woźniki to see where I had spent almost two years in hiding. we stopped at the ponds. First we visited the bunker in the dike and then the other bunkers in the forest. Not only had I aged; so had the forest. Towering trees had replaced the saplings. Michael was keyed up. Now, he said, he could imagine what we had endured. Until then he had had to rely on my descriptions only. We returned to the road and I retold the story of the last few hours before the liberation. From a distance I showed my wife and son the field where we had hidden among the grain and the place where Berl had died.

We returned to Łosice before setting out for Polinów to see the hideout in Zabiniak's pigsty. After traveling about a third of a mile I pointed to the field where, in the summer of 1941, a gendarme had trained his dog, with me as the target. The soldier had ordered me to stand behind the trees and ordered the dog to find me. Afterwards, he led me to the field and ordered me to run, or he would sick the dog on me. From then on, I checked the street carefully each time to make sure this soldier was nowhere near.

Two policemen stopped us on our way back. They inspected my driver's license and asked no questions, but left an unpleasant taste in my mouth. After having no dealings with police for so many years, why must we encounter them again?

The Jewish cemetery, along the River Toczna, had been transformed into a handsome municipal park. We entered it via Siedlce Street and I recited Kaddish. The Germans had uprooted the gravestones; even today some of them can be found lying in a heap near Dr. Wroblewski's house on the road to Niemojki, where they serve as a fence.

At the market square in Łosice I got into conversation with several locals, while Michael took pictures. Suddenly a middle-aged man approached, drunkenly asked Michael whether he had a permit to take pictures, and tried to grab the camera out of his hands. Michael did not understand a word he said. The situation became increasingly unpleasant. None of the townspeople tried to stop the man. The incident put us in a different mood; I had no more desire to chat with the locals. We packed up our belongings and set out for Treblinka.

The pastoral scene on the road from Siedlce to Treblinka was totally at variance with the memories that the extermination camp had imprinted on me. The narrow asphalt road was lined on both sides with trees, cultivated fields, green pastures, and herds of cattle, plus an occasional cluster of peasants' homes, surrounded with small gardens. Closer to Treblinka, the road plunged into the forest. It was the first time in my life that I had traveled this route in an automobile; my previous trip to Treblinka had been in a freight car. The road crossed that railroad track several times.

At the entrance to the place where the camp once stood I found administration buildings, tourist offices, a kiosk, a rest area, and conveniences. We parked our car and continued on foot along a forest path. A concrete railroad station marks the location where the transports entered the camp. I found it difficult to cope with my dual identity — the tourist in the here-and-now and the person who experienced the most terrible days he had ever known, in the very same place, which now seemed so placid. The sights, sounds, and smells, so vivid in my memory, could not have been more incompatible with the tranquility, reminiscent of a forest retreat, that the place now projected. Soon we came upon an immense monument to the victims. However, I was more strongly moved by the sight of the forest of granite monuments that had been erected behind it, each monument symbolizing a Jewish community whose members had been slaughtered here. Some of those simple monuments bear the names of the towns. There are more than 100 of them, perpetuating the memory of more than 800,000 victims of annihilation — all of them Jewish.

Memories pursued one another. The hut where I had hidden and had seen my brother for the last time no longer existed. I could see the many transports and their tens of thousands of passengers, all being led to death and then to cremation. Behind the fence that ran alongside a large field, which surrounded the barracks where the workers slept, we had piled the suitcases and clothing into towering heaps for shipment to Germany. From this place, in one of the railroad cars that was packed with such clothing, two comrades and I had managed to escape from this hell. I found the monument to the Jews of Łosice. I lit a candle and recited Kaddish again.

I pointed out the location of the three mass graves to my wife and son. Although fifty-one years had passed since my stay in Treblinka, every time I see a baby I flash back to those infants who sat on the lip of the enormous grave in which the corpses were burning. I will never be able to forget that sight.

We ended the trip with a visit to my wife's birthplace, the small town of Rudnik, on the River San in southern Poland. This place, too, left a bleak impression.

After the Germans liquidated Polish Jewry, the Polish authorities sought to obscure the evidence that Jews had ever lived in that country. In many towns, Jewish cemeteries were destroyed and new buildings constructed on their ruins. Synagogues that the Germans had not destroyed became warehouses, workshops, and even movie theaters. In most of these towns, as in Łosice, memorial plaques commemorating the thousands of Jewish inhabitants whom the Nazis had murdered had vanished. But memorial plaques for Poles whom the Germans had killed stood there prominently. Not all blood is equal, just as the Nazis claimed....

Appendix A
*After the Liberation — a Letter**

September 1939 my cousin Rachel with a lot of people made their way east towards the Russian occupied part of Poland. In the spring of 1940, they were sent to Siberia. July 31, 1944, when the Russian army was advancing over the Bug river and our town was a liberated, she started writing letters to her family, but no answer came. Then she sent a letter to the pharmacist who was Polish and lived across the street. He gave the letter to my father.

In this letter I am telling her what happened.

Dear cousin,

My dear, I received your letter and was very delighted to read it. You cannot imagine how happy I was when the Lieutenant handed me the letter, the letter I had been hoping to receive for five years, the letter that allowed me to hope that someone close, to whom I can write a few words, has survived after all. That hope is you — my only cousin — because I still have no idea whether any other member of my family has survived. My dear, I know that the letter you received from me must have caused you much disappointment and sadness, since I told the whole truth and left nothing out. I decided to tell you the whole truth because otherwise it would be worse for you and

* When I wrote this letter I did not know of any other death camps. Auschwitz was liberated a couple of weeks later.

harder for me. I write these lines with a heavy heart, knowing how much pain they will cause you when I tell you how your closest family members were murdered. Rachel, it would be much easier if I could cry as I write these lines, but I cannot. My heart has become as hard as molten steel that is poured into cold water. I cannot cry for my pain.

My dear, you wrote that you would try to send me some money. Thank you very much, but I don't need money. If I had a way, I would send you many thousands, as much as you ask, because I still have money left over from Treblinka. In addition, Father, who visits me every two weeks, brings me as much money as I want since he is making a good living as a tailor.

So, my dear, I will begin by describing our lives in Łosice under German rule. From early 1939 until December 1, 1941, the Germans murdered Jews on the basis of their Jewishness only, whereas the others managed somehow to live. People aged 12-60 were sent to slave labor at a location near the forest, or to a camp. On December 1, 1941, the ghetto was established in our Łosice. This is how matters looked: all the Jews were packed into a very cramped area, each apartment shared by several families. At all the entrances to the ghetto, signs were posted with the following message on the side facing outside: "Entering the ghetto is forbidden due to typhus epidemic." On the side facing in, the following was written: "Leaving the ghetto is forbidden. Violators will be executed." One of the first victims who died in the ghetto was old Miriam-Rivka. Jews were given a ration of 75 grams (2.5 ounces) of bread per day, distributed on the basis of coupons. That's how the mass murder began. When autumn came and the weather turned cold, people died like flies. That's how they killed us until August 22, 1942. My father was taken to a labor camp in Siedlce in June 1942. Then came Saturday, August 22, a day I will remember forever, a sad day. All the residents of the ghetto were assembled in the market square. Carts were brought to the square for the women and children; the men had to run. After we crossed the second bridge on the way to Siedlce they began shooting from behind us. We didn't know where they were leading us, because our county was almost the first in Poland where these things were happening. There were no escape attempts because everyone wanted to stay together with his family. So they prodded us forward, shooting from behind, all the way to Siedlce. There they took us to a square where everyone from the Siedlce and Mordy ghettos had already been gathered. We sat there, under SS fire, until 3 o'clock. At 3 o'clock Saturday afternoon, we were made to run to the railroad platform. There we sat again until Sunday. On Monday at 11 o'clock we were loaded into the cars, 150-200 people per car. My dear, I would not wish such a situation on anyone, except for our enemies. We had no water. My dear, a person may need water even more than food. I came to that realization when I saw people slurping water from sewage ditches because it was so hot.

I stayed close to my Srulik and to Mottl's family, having already been separated from my mother on the way to Siedlce. That is where I saw her for the last time, walking behind a cart. Yes, Rachel, even these few incomprehensible words are so difficult for me to write.

We were taken to Treblinka, the Treblinka where three and a half million Jews were exterminated.* Ega and Malka's Noah, Aunt Leah, Bracha and her son Chaim, and Rivka — members of Mottl's family — were together with me there. Mottl himself was no longer with us because he had been shot in the square at Siedlce.

We were taken to Treblinka, and in that hellhole Srulik and I were selected for labor. Our job was to empty the railroad cars of the people who had suffocated to death on the way. Only 20 percent of the passengers reached Treblinka alive. I reached the inferno on August 24, and the next day, August 25, as I waited in line for water (only two pails of water were brought for thousands of people), I was shot in the chest, on the right side. My brother tried to help me, and while still conscious I saw blood spurting from my chest and back. I tried to move closer and end my life — because I saw that they were murdering even healthy people — but my brother burst into tears. My brother saved me and concealed me in a hut among piles of rags. Afterwards, he went out to bring me water and never returned. That is how I parted from my only brother forever.

My dear, you are asking too much of me. I know this letter will cost you in terms of health, but I have to tell you everything.

* For the sake of historical precision, we should note that about 870,000 Jews were murdered in Treblinka.

On September 9, I escaped from that inferno together with two of my friends. After the first few days [in Treblinka], I crawled out of the shack where I was hiding to see if any of my relatives were still alive. After hours of searching I found a familiar face. I approached him and asked him if he, too, was from Łosice. He answered in the affirmative. He was the son of Shaya Rosenzweig, the builder. I asked him if anyone else from our town had survived, and he answered that seven had survived along with him, and no more. I escaped with him and another man. We slipped into a car that set out with victims' clothing. In Treblinka, they murdered people with poison gas.

My father was still at the camp in Siedlce. I went there and you can imagine what my reunion with Father was like. I took him to Łosice, because at that time a ghetto had been established there for people who held permits to work in the villages. I also worked but I went home at night. We stayed in the second ghetto until November 22, 1942. That day, we went into hiding on a farm and lived in a pigsty, under the pigs. We stayed there for only twenty days because the peasant who concealed us began tp be afraid.

I still have enough money from Treblinka. You can imagine how much it was if I still have cash two years later.

On December 19, we moved to a bunker near the fishponds. There were four of us. One of them was a barber who had been deported; another was the son of Peretz the baker, named Berko. Try to imagine how we lived there. Everyone was searching for us — Poles of the People's

Army (the Armia Krajowa), the Germans, and the Germans' Ukrainian lackeys. We could not join the partisans because bandits from the People's Army, ostensibly partisans who had come from London, were swarming around us. On November 27, 1942, Łosice was cleansed of Jews.

We could not cook in the bunker. We cooked in the forest at night because no one could come out during the day. We lived that way for two years. Sometimes we could not buy bread, even for a gold coin. On April 13, 1944, workers from the Woźniki estate, the place where we had made our "home," discovered us. The only thing we wanted was to survive, not to live well, just to be able to avenge all our sufferings.

Berko, Peretz's son, was shot to death one day before the Red Army arrived. We came out of the forest because the Germans had surrounded it with artillery and began looking for us in the Woźniki fields. Father hid in a pile of grain; the German who searched for him on the other side pushed several sheaves aside but did not see him even though Father's footprints led to the sheaves. I lay some distance away as they killed Peretz's son. This happened on July 30, 1944.

The next day, July 31, we were liberated. That day, two hours before the Red Army came in, Germans captured me and Father and took us to their commander. I explained to him that we were Poles, but they screamed that we were Russians, *ivanii*. Think of it, my dear: to face our last moment an hour before the liberation, after all the suffering and agonies we had endured.

I don't know why they let us go. If they had asked for our papers, we had nothing to show them. I spoke to them in German — I had learned the language in the bunker by reading German newspapers, and to speak it, too. I led them to understand that we were heading back to work when the artillery fire began. We looked for shelter in the field of rye, and that's where they found us. They held us for forty-five minutes, and when they let us go, we crawled into the pond under the heavy German fire. After we lay there for about half an hour, I saw five soldiers approach us, stooping. I thought they were German soldiers. Even with liberation so imminent, I could not believe that these were liberators. I stood up to show them the way to the bridge. I wanted to show them that I was not afraid. I pointed out the way. I saw four of them leaping over the trench and the officer approaching us. I saw that his epaulettes were not the German type. He turned to me: "Where have the Germans gone?" Father said that we did not know because we were not from this area. He turned to walk away, but some natural urge opened my mouth. "Are you Russian?" I asked him. *Da*, he replied. Imagine that moment, my dear. We smothered him with kisses. He was a captain in the Russian army, and he calmed us by saying, "Don't be afraid of anyone, because we are with you."

That's how our agonies came to an end. Only then, however, were we aware of whom and what we had lost. Only then did our hearts begin to ache for those who had perished. Until then, we had been preoccupied only with our own survival. My dear, I tell you all this only so you may understand how things were.

Dear cousin, the newspaper must have told you how the Jews were murdered, but everything you read is only a drop in the ocean in comparison with what happened. I am sure this letter will shock you, but after all, you are no longer a little girl. It's all over, done with, vanished, never to return. We will have to get used to our fate.

My dear — in regard to your sister and father, I can only tell you that I have not seen them since the day we were deported from Łosice.

Sarah Gittl had already had a second child by that time. Yankl did everything he could to bring food home. Your father was living with Sarah Gittl then and so were your sister and her husband. Esther Yocheved, together with her husband Srulik and their children, were in Siedlce until the last day.

I have nothing more of importance to tell you here. At this point, then, I conclude this letter, which has cost me no small amount of health. I had to stop writing several times because I had a headache. I enclose a photograph of your father.

I wish you, your family, and your friends all the best. I kiss you from afar.

Yidl Weinstein

I sent you my picture about a month ago. In my next letter, my dear, I will send you the names of the survivors from Łosice.

Appendix B

Generations of Jewish Life in Łosice: The Author's Overview of His Town

Between the two world wars, the town of Łosice, one of many towns of similar size in central Poland, had thousands of inhabitants. Łosice is on the right-hand bank of the Toczna, a tributary of the River Bug. The town is on a plain that is punctuated here and there by hills and many rivulets. Forests with variegated vegetation still grow along the Toczna near the Bug, where the land has been cultivated for generations. The verdure of the cultivated fields and the pastures extends to the outskirts of town.

Two roads run through Łosice. One connects Siedlce with Biala Podlaska; the other links Miedzyrzec-Podlask and Sokolów. The market square is in the center of town. The main streets from the square are named for the localities to which they lead.

Shortly before the twentieth century began, a railroad was built from Western Europe to Tsarist Russia, via Warsaw. That brought Łosice closer to the big world, although the nearest railroad station was in Niemojki, about three miles away. Much later, elderly inhabitants of Łosice related that Russian railroad engineers seemed willing to build a line in the vicinity of Łosice, for a "commission" of several thousand rubles, but since the inhabitants could not afford such luxuries, the track bypassed the Niemojki station, which remains intact decades later. Freight and even people continued to travel by cart all the way to Warsaw, 75 miles away. It was less expensive to do things that way and it obviated the need to load and unload. Time did not mean very much back then.

In the early Middle Ages, the area was on the border between the sovereign territories of two royal dynasties: the Piasts in Mazovia (Mazowsze) and Gediminas in Lithuania. As Lithuania expanded in later centuries, Ruthenians (from Little Russia) and Poles settled the area intensively. To this day the names of many localities include Lacki (Polish) or Ruski (Ruthenian), denoting the ethnic affiliation of their original inhabitants. There are also ruins and remnants of Greek Orthodox churches from bygone times.

Poles began to constitute a majority during the period of the Jagiellonian kings (1386-1572); Poland annexed the entire area before 1500. Eventually, all the Ruthenians left, making the area entirely Polish Catholic, as it remains to this day. The only remnants of the Ruthenian past are names from previous centuries that exist in the census records in Łosice.

Although there is no evidence for it, it stands to reason that Łosice, which was established under Lithuanian law, existed in the Middle Ages. The oldest document that mentions Łosice explicitly is the Locality Law of 1505, which was signed in Radom by King Alexander Jagiello. The earliest document that mentions Jews in Łosice is from twenty years later, during the reign of Sigismund I the Old. Meir Esofovich, an affluent Jew from Brest-Litovsk, acquired the right to operate customs offices in several outlying towns in Podlasie County, including Łosice.

Some Jews who settled in the county came from western Poland, along with Poles from the same area. Many others, however, came straight from Germany, where they had been persecuted during the religious wars and fled the anti-Jewish violence that accompanied the hostilities. The Polish monarch and the large estate owners were pleased with the Jewish newcomers, whom they saw as burghers who could stimulate the development of commerce. In the middle of the seventeenth century, chroniclers noted a flow of Jewish escapees to Podlasie from countries that had been overrun by Chmielnicki's hordes.

Documents indicate that living conditions in Łosice were always harsh. The townspeople pleaded with the king for protection from abuses of power by the *starosta* (royal county governors) and petitioned for extra privileges — to hold fairs, to be exempted from various taxes, and to make and sell alcoholic beverages.

A document from the second half of the seventeenth century, signed by King John III Sobieski, contains a ruling on a suit filed by inhabitants of Łosice alleging unfair commercial competition by the Jews. The document shows that long before that time the Jewish community in Łosice was considered permanent.

Łosice withered because of its distance from the main crossroads. It still served as an administrative and commercial center of sorts and supported itself on the services of artisans in nearby villages. However, many of its residents worked in agriculture. A small processed food industry gradually developed, based on local produce. There were breweries and distilleries in Łosice, along with flourmills, rendering plants for edible oils, tanneries, and dairies. Since time immemorial the town had regular markets and annual fairs. At one time, Łosice was known far and wide for its horse market. It was natural for Jews to take part in the local economy. Utilizing relations with fellow Jews in distant towns, they quickly became exporters of farm produce. Via Węgrow, which had an older, wealthier, and larger Jewish community, they sold grain to localities as distant as Gdansk. However, unrest at that time — mainly due to the Cossack uprisings, the Swedish invasions, and civil war — disrupted economic stability throughout Podlasie County. All the towns in the area, including Łosice, began to languish. During the wars with Sweden, the town was torched and its population decimated. Only during the lengthy reign of the last king of Poland, Stanisław-August Poniatowski, did Łosice recover slightly.

Even that resurgence was short-lived. In the partitioning of Poland, Podlasie County was rent in two — part annexed by Russia, the rest by Austria. The annexation led to economic stagnation. Several years later, Łosice was incorporated into the Grand Duchy of Warsaw. During that brief interlude, Poles dreamed about the resurrection of Greater Poland, while the Jews hoped that Napoleon's soldiers would announce their emancipation. In fact, the retreating remnants of the Grande Armée left behind nothing save for memories of rape and looting. As always, civilians paid the price of the wars.

In Łosice, the era of foreign rule in Poland, punctuated by three armed insurrections, was in no sense a time of prosperity. The entire town, built of wood, burned to the ground twice during the nineteenth century. Each time, the townsfolk had to relocate to neighboring towns or the forest, where they lived in tents or dugouts until their homes were rebuilt. Only after the second conflagration did most inhabitants start building their houses of brick.

The processes of industrialization and the development of transport left Łosice largely unaffected. Unlike Warsaw or Białystok, Podlasie County was hardly touched by economic progress. The only exception was Siedlce. Although established long after Łosice, it became the county seat and a major rail junction.

The percent of Jews in the population of Łosice before the nineteenth century cannot be estimated. Censuses from the nineteenth century estimate their share at one-half. By 1921, this figure climbed to 70 percent. Shortly before World War II, almost 5,000 of Łosice's 6,000 inhabitants were Jewish. They lived in congested conditions on the market square and along the main streets. Most of them were petty merchants or artisans. Some families had small shops that were passed on from generation to generation and served customers from the entire district. Other local Jews were wholesale merchants who purchased grain and other produce from the peasants, stored it in their own warehouses, and resold it in the cities. More substantial dealers had agents to buy for them.

As the prospects of upward social mobility diminished, young people began to embrace innumerable novel ideas. With the possible exception of assimilationism, the range of political and social views held by Jews in Łosice was no different from that held by Jews in Warsaw. Social-democratic groups had existed since the nineteenth century and many wage laborers joined the Bund. During the Russian Revolution of 1905, the Bund organized strikes and demonstrations. Later, between the world wars, some young people rushed to join leftist organizations and others supported Zionist groups. Both circles had their share of extremists and idealists. Lecturers from out of town were invited to speak at libraries and before drama groups. Many youngsters attended summer camps, where they formed friendships with their peers from elsewhere in the county. Although these young Jews had little formal schooling, most were quite sophisticated and familiar with the new political and social ideas that had been making large inroads among both Jewish and Polish literary groups.

Jews of middle age were connected to their *shtiblakh* (small, intimate synagogues), which tended to be differentiated by the worshippers' occupation. The elderly followed the lead of well-known rabbis in other towns and aligned themselves with separate groups. The rabbis of Konstantinów, Kock, and Radzyn all had followers in Łosice.

Parents did what they could to arrange employment for their offspring, mainly out of concern that otherwise their children would stray from the straight path. However, apprentices were unpaid. Often things worked the other way around: those who taught a trade while enjoying the youngster's free labor actually demanded payment from the worker's parents for their efforts.

Many Łosice Jews hoped to move elsewhere. Before World War I, the destinations of choice were the United States and Canada. Letters from emigrés fired townspeople's imagination. Despite their dreadful poverty in the New World, Jewish emigrés adjusted quickly because, after Łosice, economic hardship seemed normal to them. Their letters described a new life in which people were valued not for their lineage, but their achievements, irrespective of religious affiliation. This was a tremendous novelty in Łosice, where Jews had always seen themselves as outsiders and were used to being humiliated. No wonder they felt the urge to leave.

When World War I ended, the Jewish population experienced a sense of relief. It proved to be short-lived as General Józef Haller's Polish nationalist battalions began to harass "foreigners." The war that broke out with

Bolshevik Russia made matters worse because the Polish authorities considered the Jews to be natural allies of the enemy. After the Russians retreated, several local Jews were prosecuted for collaboration but acquitted for lack of evidence.

In the 1920s, the United States imposed immigration quotas and emigration to that country became more difficult. A few enterprising individuals attempted to get away to South America or Western Europe and did not always adhere to legalities. Zionist organizations inspired young people to hope to reach Palestine; those who wished to go always outnumbered the supply of visas to that country. So the vast majority of Łosice Jews stayed behind. They had no choice.